Manage the Message

by

Bryan Thresher and Jim Biggin

CENTURY
BUSINESS

Copyright © Bryan Thresher and Jim Biggin 1993

The right of Bryan Thresher and Jim Biggin to be identified as the authors of this work has been asserted by them in accordance with the Copyright, Designs and Patents Act, 1988.

First published in the UK 1993
by Century Business
An imprint of Random House UK Ltd
20 Vauxhall Bridge Road, London SW1V 2SA

Random House Australia (Pty) Ltd
20 Alfred Street, Milsons Point
Sydney, NSW 2061, Australia

Random House New Zealand Ltd
18 Poland Road, Glenfield
Auckland 10, New Zealand

Random House South Africa (Pty) Ltd
PO Box 337, Bergvlei, South Africa

Set in Bembo by SX Composing Ltd, Rayleigh, Essex
Printed and bound in Great Britain by
Mackays of Chatham PLC, Chatham, Kent

A catalogue record for this book is available from the British Library.

ISBN 0-7126-5681-2

Contents

Acknowledgements

Sincere thanks are owed to:

Everybody who suggested we write this book. Mike Simpson for help and criticism. Tina Sweetland for casting a manager's sceptical eye over the draft. Jenny Alderman, for her expert advice and guidance as a management development consultant.

Associated Newspapers Ltd and Financial Times Syndication for permission to quote extracts from *The Daily Mail* and *Financial Times* respectively in the chapter on Articulation.

And, of course, to Angela and Maureen, for their faith and patience. This book is dedicated to them.

Times and Helvetica are trademarks of Linotype AG and/or its subsidiaries. ITC Zapf Chancery is a trademark of the International Typeface Corporation.

About the authors

Both authors are professional communicators.

Bryan Thresher has a Cambridge degree in languages. He spent over twenty years in sales and marketing management positions with leading international computer companies. For the last eight years, he has been a consultant, specialising in information technology market research, marketing planning and training.

He is active in local community affairs, and in his spare time, he writes for pleasure. (It can't be for the money!)

Jim Biggin has twenty-five years experience in sales, marketing and general management. He has worked for large multinationals and small entrepreneurial companies in both the insurance and computer sectors. He is now an insurance management consultant, and has designed several management training courses.

His hobbies include bridge and golf. He is not particularly communicative about his handicap . . .

Introduction

Manage the Message is about helping you to use writing to achieve your goals. Specifically, it will show you how to use written communications to motivate others. It will:

1. **Give you a practical and methodical approach to developing persuasive arguments**
2. **Help you express these arguments effectively**

THE DOLPHIN

This book is based on a workshop we regularly hold. At the beginning of each workshop, we project a photograph of a dolphin leaping into the air out of a clear blue ocean. We ask course members what they see. All say 'a dolphin'. Some add something like 'a sense of power, grace and beauty'. One or two (and sometimes none at all) go on to say 'a brilliant photograph', and comment on the use of a telephoto lens, a fast shutter, the tight depth of field and so on.

At this point, our students wonder what on earth this has to do with using written communications to motivate people. We then explain as follows:

- **The photographer made the picture.** He or she understood what techniques to use in order to create the image he or she wanted. The photographer knew exactly what effect a telephoto lens and a fast shutter would have, and cropped the print to suit the subject. Motivating people through written communication is exactly the same. It is not a talent we are all born with. It involves skills and techniques which have to be learned. This book will help you become aware of these techniques, how they work, and how they can be used.

- **The photographer didn't make the dolphin.** We are working with real people in a real world. We do not tell you how to invent arguments which do not exist. We show you how to spot the arguments, and how to organise and present them so that you can achieve your own particular objectives.

PERSUASION

This book will add an important skill to your inventory. How many times have you watched a new opportunity being missed, simply because no one knew how to sell the idea to others? Many of us are employed because we have some special knowledge or experience, and our employers rely on us to recommend a particular course of action when a problem needs solving. This investment, however, is largely wasted if nobody acts on our judgement. Most of us are in the business of working with others to get things done, and nowadays this involves persuasion rather than direction. This applies not only to people and companies with whom we do business, but also to people who work with us. Anybody who relies on others doing something 'because it's their job' was definitely born forty years too late. In most situations, we have to do a 'selling job' to make things happen.

How do we learn to 'sell'? We can, of course, go on sales training courses or buy books on the subject, but these are mainly about getting orders from customers. They talk about mysterious things such as 'openers' and 'scripts' to grab attention, 'getting agreement early', 'handling objections' and 'preference closes'. These things are not especially useful when we're trying to motivate our colleagues, or to alert management to a problem or a new business opportunity. Indeed, to the sensitive souls among us, sales techniques in these situations appear forced and intrusive. We can shut the door on a double glazing salesman, but could we really face this sort of thing every day at the office?

Fortunately, there is another way, as you will see.

EFFECTIVE WRITING

How many times have you seen a serious mistake being made, only to discover that the information which could have prevented it was there all the time? Somebody already knew, but the vital piece of information never left his or her desk. Or perhaps it did, but nobody noticed, because the message was badly expressed and never understood.

There are many reasons for failures in communication, but (aside from telepathy) written communication is more prone to disaster than any other medium. The reason is that when we meet face-to-face or phone, we get a stream of instant feedback which tells us how the conversation is going. What our listeners say to us, the tone of their voice, and (when we are meeting) the look in their eye, nods, shakes of the head, the shrug of the shoulders, all these things give us valuable clues which keep us on track. Such body language is easy to interpret: after all, it's something we learned as toddlers. When we write, however, we do not have the benefit of feedback. There is nothing to stop us writing baffling, confusing, and poorly-presented material guaranteed to bore or annoy the reader. Some of us do just that, and pay the price.

This sort of experience can put us off the whole idea of writing. Many of us find the job of writing so hard and potentially dangerous that we give up, and reach for the phone or ask for a meeting instead. Our readers may find our report so obscure that they do exactly the same thing. There are very good reasons for meeting or phoning (as we shall see), but evading the responsibility of writing isn't one of them. We can all recall meetings which wasted many work-hours in an attempt to cover matters which we knew could have been dealt with more effectively in writing. Don't forget that the early part of most meetings is spent talking about the weather, the roadworks on the motorway, so-and-so's promotion, or on recapping for the benefit of the one person who was not at the last meeting. Or it may happen the other way round. We have all travelled to meetings where the formal agenda has been polished off in a few minutes. What do we do then? We feel guilty that we've spent two hours travelling to a ten-minute meeting, so we prolong the proceedings, just to keep our consciences quiet. How's that for productivity?

In any event, as we operate throughout the single EC market, we find we can't always meet (because of the cost of travel) or phone (because of the language problem). Written communications can be translated, but we can hardly expect someone to translate our phone call in advance. Whether we like it or not, much of what we want to say to our EC colleagues has to be said in writing.

There are, of course, plenty of books on 'effective writing', but these explain how to present an argument clearly and grammatically. They do not explain how to develop the persuasive argument in the first place.

Manage The Message is unique in that it covers the key elements of being persuasive and effective writing. To use an old analogy, if effective writing is about carving stones, *Manage The Message* is about building cathedrals.

FORTUNATELY . . .

There are a couple of things about written communication which will make our task easier. The first is that we have the time to think about what we're trying to achieve, and to change our ideas as we go through the drafting process. We have all come away from meetings or phone calls and kicked ourselves. 'Why on earth didn't I say that . . ?' When writing, we have more time to cover all the angles beforehand.

Second, we can learn by example. Few of us have the chance to watch good negotiators or sales professionals in action, but we can all learn to spot examples of good writing all around us in newspapers and quality magazines. On the other hand, advertising copy in local newspapers and some of the junk mail which falls through our letterboxes are both rich sources of illustrations of how not to do it.

This book, then, will show you how to *manage* the ways in which you use writing to deal with your colleagues, your suppliers and your customers. It will enhance your job prospects by showing you how to achieve your objectives while at the same time helping others to reach theirs. In other words, how to succeed without losing your friends.

AND . . .

There are also two or three important spin-offs. First, being able to communicate your expertise and motivate others will boost your self-confidence. Once you have applied the techniques described in this book a few times and seen what they can do, they will become automatic. You will acquire the key skill of putting yourself in the other person's shoes. The whole of this book is based upon this simple trick. All the methodologies and techniques it contains are designed to help you see the world from the other's point of view, and to show you how you can use this special ability to achieve your aims. You will enjoy using it, and you'll find yourself thinking about the world in a rather different way. Problems will become challenges, and they'll be challenges that you know you can handle.

Second, although the book is mainly about written communication, many of the lessons about building persuasive arguments also apply to oral communication. If you use the techniques, not only will your written messages improve, but you will also find it easier to plan important phone calls or put together key presentations.

Third, your profile will become much higher when you communicate effectively. Like most other things in life, we enjoy doing what we do well, and the more we enjoy it, the more often we do it. People will remember you, not only for your special area of expertise, but also as a fertile source of ideas, and as someone who knows how to get results. The person who is promoted is often the one who readily comes to mind, in the same way that we only use the bits we can see when we're trying to complete a jigsaw puzzle. If others know you're there, what you can do, and where to find you, you will become the next piece to fit into the puzzle.

BUT NOT . . .

There are a few things the book will not do. It will not force you into a straitjacket, so that your writing becomes stereotyped 'standard' business English. On the contrary, you will find that the techniques will encourage you to use your imagination and express your own personality.

Neither do we spend time on grammar and spelling. You can buy other books which hand out stern lectures on tautologies and split infinitives, and you can always use a spell-checker to catch your 'compatable's and 'supercede's.

Another thing the book will not do is tell you how to manipulate others against their will. At several points, we make it clear that if what you're trying to do is not to others' advantage, then you will fail. The book's big message is that you can get your way while others also get theirs.

Finally, it cannot force you to use the skills. You can flip through this book, maybe smile here and there, and carry on as before. Or you can read, think, remember the key points, and try the suggested techniques to see whether they work for you. Bearing in mind the short time it takes to read the book, the effort will have been worth it even if it only helps you produce one good report or important sales proposal.

BY THE WAY . . .

The book contains some 'war stories' in order to illustrate particular points. Some may make you laugh or weep, and a good number will stretch your credulity. We assure you that they are all, without exception, based on real incidents which we have witnessed. In many instances, the stories do not show those involved in a particularly flattering light, so we have sometimes disguised the identities of individuals and organisations to save the guilty from further embarrassment.

Good luck, and put it in writing!

Bryan Thresher   Jim Biggin.

1. The 10A Technique

In this first chapter, we shall present a couple of ideas which we shall be using throughout the book to make things clearer, the 'Goblin' and the 'tribe'. We shall also introduce you to the basic 10A planning technique, and show what it can do.

MEET THE GOBLIN, MSc.

'The Goblin' is the arch enemy you never knew you had! Everybody you write to has a Goblin sitting on their shoulder and whispering in their ear.

The Goblin works for the paper industry, so he devotes 80 per cent of his time to trying to increase consumption of paper. The other 20 per cent he devotes to his hobby – damaging your career. He does this by deliberately misunderstanding everything you write.

When his human receives a letter, memo, report, sales proposal (in fact, anything in writing), he whispers things like:

**"What on earth is all this about?
Crikey! This is complicated.
Who is this guy anyway?
Can we trust him?
What in heaven's name does he
    expect us to do about it?
Don't you think that's a bit risky?
Don't you have enough to worry
    about already?
I would deal with this later if I
    were you.
Pass it on to someone else . . .
Bin it!"**

He is, of course, a figment of our imagination. But we'd like him to become a figment of yours too.

As we mentioned earlier, one of the problems with writing is that we don't have feedback from our audience in the way we do when we meet or speak on the phone. So the Goblin is there to give us just that kind of feedback. Instead of writing in a vacuum to some faceless person, it helps if we can predict the kind of sarcastic comments or objections that a bloody-minded reader will come up with. Hence the Goblin. The MSc? 'Master of Scepticism,' of course.

He'll be popping up every now and then during the book to remind us he's there, and to let us know when we start going wrong. He'll be helping us see things from the reader's point of view.

THE 'TRIBE' CONCEPT

We all operate in one or more 'tribes' each with its own goals, values, reference points and ways of doing things. The way we behave will differ, depending on which particular tribe we happen to be living with.

For instance, 'family', 'business' and 'local community' are three tribes that most of us belong to.

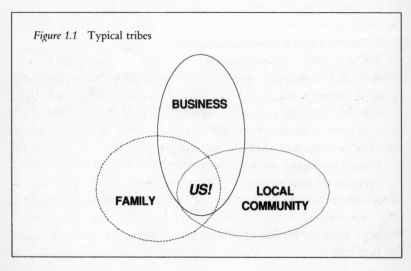

Figure 1.1   Typical tribes

We do not, however, behave in the same way in each. The way we act in the privacy of our own home would not be appropriate in the office (and vice versa, of course). We all know that young children need to be treated rather differently from the way we deal with our business colleagues. Then, of course, we will have yet another set of behaviour reserved for our friends and neighbours.

These examples are simple, but the same applies in business life. 'Our organisation' might be regarded as a tribe, complete with its own set of objectives, procedures, structures and relationships. 'Our department' is also a tribe, a smaller one within the organisation tribe. Our customer belongs to his or her own 'tribe', and so does our supplier.

When we are dealing with people within our own tribe, communication and motivation is easy, because most individuals understand clearly what is involved and what each of us wants, for instance:

From: Phil
To: Pat

Have a look at the attached and do the necessary, will you?

No explanation was needed in this memo, since both parties understood it clearly.

When we move *outside* our tribe, however, we have to take into account different tribal customs. This applies when handling customers or suppliers, or when we are working for 'Manufacturing' and we need something from 'Personnel' – or when, as middle managers, we are dealing with top management. If we fail to change our approach, there is little chance of our argument being persuasive or even understood, and we will simply be overruled or ignored.

This, of course, is one of the reasons why many of us have a shock when we're promoted to head up a department for the first time. We suddenly discover that things have changed. Until now, we have been shielded from inter-tribal warfare, but now we have the responsibility of representing our department's interests in the teeth of opposition from other departments. At the same time, we have just been appointed to the management tribe, and we are expected to represent this tribe when dealing with former colleagues. In both cases, we find that all our tried and trusted means of persuasion no longer work, and we have to find new ones.

Problems can arise when we get our tribes mixed up. To assume that Marketing and Customer Engineering both work within the same 'company' tribe is asking for trouble. In all the companies we ever worked for, they were two distinct tribes. And we have all been fogged at one time or another with computer jargon from the IT people. Or maybe Accounts sent us a horrendous printout of numbers with a little note in the margin saying, 'I thought you should be aware'. They are making the natural, but totally misplaced, assumption that we speak their tribal language.

To make matters worse, tribes can overlap. This very often happens in organisations with 'matrix management structures'. Let us say we're in Central Marketing, and we have a marketing lady in Paris reporting to us on a dotted line. How she will react to us will depend upon whether the tribal head-dress she's wearing at that moment is from her 'Marketing' tribe or her 'France' tribe.

The 'different tribe' problem is bad enough when we're meeting, but at least then we get a feel for where we're going wrong, and when to change tack. When we're writing, the pitfalls are that much easier to stumble into. We may never even realise we fell in.

In summary, then, when we're dealing with people who are not members of our own tribe, we have to stop and think very carefully.

Jim has a story about this.

For some years I sold insurance. Among other things, this involved walking unannounced into public houses to meet the publican. The first time I tried this, I marched in dressed in a sharp business suit. Unfortunately, he immediately recognised the dress of the Customs & Excise tribe, and assumed that I was a roving VAT inspector. It took a fair bit of hard work on my part to rescue the situation.

Next time, I switched to a smart blazer with grey trousers and casually ambled in. The publican now thought he recognised a member of his customer tribe, and beamed a friendly welcome. However, when he realised I was a salesman, his face darkened in suspicion. I was still in disguise!

The third time, I hit upon the publican's idea of the correct dress for the salesmen tribe. The blazer and grey trousers were fine, but I had to wave the spear of the salesman, a briefcase. Bingo! He knew why I was there, and how to greet me. Both of us were happy as we set about trading beads.

We don't have to join the other tribe, we just need to know how to work with it . . .

THE 10A TECHNIQUE

Many of us may have acquired an intuitive way of tackling the problem of working with other tribes, but all of us can benefit from extra help. The 10A Technique offers a structured approach. It invites us to think about a number of key issues when we're working with another tribe, and offers a set of guidelines to help us get it consistently right.

It is a kind of toolkit which enables us to spot the right arguments, and to anticipate queries, misunderstandings, disagreements and reluctance to make decisions. The 10A Technique is our main weapon against the Goblin; a checklist containing all the things we need to think about when we're planning a communication. If you write regularly, you may find you already think about at least some of the elements it contains. On the other hand, the list may come as a complete surprise. Either way, it's to be used as a kind of framework for organising your ideas *before* you put pen to paper or finger to keyboard.

1. **Aims** (the operational objective to which the communication will contribute)

2. **Action** (the intended effect of the communication)

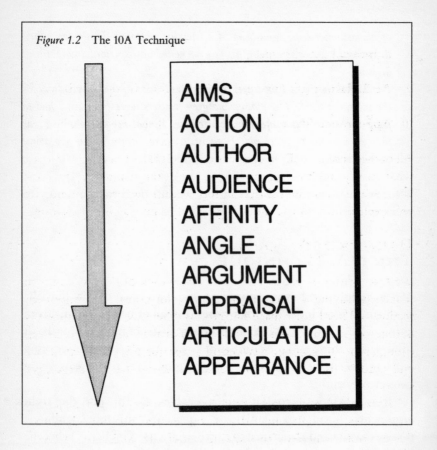

Figure 1.2 The 10A Technique

AIMS
ACTION
AUTHOR
AUDIENCE
AFFINITY
ANGLE
ARGUMENT
APPRAISAL
ARTICULATION
APPEARANCE

3. **Author** (the sender of the communication)

4. **Audience** (the recipients of the communication)

5. **Affinity** (the motivating connection between the author and the audience)

6. **Angle** (the point of view to be adopted)

7. **Argument** (the outline content of the communication)

8. **Appraisal** (checkpoint)

9. **Articulation** (the way the communication is expressed)

10. **Appearance** (the physical appearance of the communication)

All of these points will, in one way or another, have a direct effect on what we say and how we say it. The rest of the chapters in the book will cover each of the subjects in more detail. For the moment, we will explain how to use the 10A list, and to give a simple example.

USING A 10A FORM

We take a sheet of paper, and write down each of the 'A' points in sequence, leaving a space under each one for notes. The Argument section will need most space since this is where we'll be building the outline of our case. (The sample 10A Form in the Appendix has enough space to generate a two-page letter: for a detailed report, we will need to use one or more additional sheets for the Argument section.)

As we think about each of the points in order, we will be jotting down notes, not only under that particular heading, but others too. For example, when we're thinking about the Audience, we may decide that it's our customer's managing director we need to write to. We write 'MD' under the Audience heading. He is a busy person, so we had better not sent him a tome to wade through. So under Articulation, we jot down 'Single page – 'informal.' The document should look professional, so under Appearance we note 'Times – full letterhead.' (Don't worry what some of these things mean for the moment: it's the principle we're explaining.) Then we go back and carry on with the next point, Affinity, and so on through the list.

When we come to Argument, we build an outline of what we plan to say, and then go to a built-in checkpoint, Appraisal. This is where we pause to make sure we haven't given the audience any cause to question our reasoning, such as making unwarranted assumptions. To complete the form, we add any other points which may have occurred to us about Articulation and Appearance. We then start drafting the final communication.

In practice, applying the 10A Technique takes from 10 to 30 minutes – depending upon the length and complexity of the document – but the end result will be a communication which works.

Example: the 10A Technique in action

Assume you are the Quality Assurance Manager for the Basingstoke Building Society. This is a new appointment, and your job is to handle customer complaints which have found their way on to the desk of the Society's Chief Executive. You have noticed a particular problem with the Winchester branch. Over the last few months, there have been a large number of complaints about the appearance of the branch premises; 'dirty', 'disgracefully untidy', 'litter everywhere', 'chewing gum on one of the writing pads' are some of the things you've been reading. The procedure is for you to write formally to the branch to correct the problem. Your first instinct may be to write something like:

From: T. Smith, QA
To: Mrs R. Jones, Branch Manager, Winchester

We are receiving a growing number of complaints about the cleanliness of your branch. Winchester branch is now top of the list in the Action Table. As branch manager, you should realise that dirty and untidy premises are not consistent with the Society's image of friendly professionalism. I would ask you therefore to take immediate steps to ensure that the appearance of the branch gives no cause for future complaints.

This might do the trick. But what might the branch manager's Goblin say?

"Who is this guy? What's QA, for goodness' sake? And what's the 'Action Table'? 'Dirty'? It's not our fault, it's the damn cleaners. Who exactly was complaining? Just who does this 'T. Smith' think he's talking to? Does he realise how many customers we have through here every day?"

Quite right too! If we had used the 10A Technique, we might have prepared a plan of the letter which would look something like the sample on the following page.

Some of the entries may look a little cryptic at this stage, but the rest of the book will explain the simple processes involved in producing such a 10A Form. The main point is that we used the 10A Technique to produce a framework for the letter and an outline of the argument.

We can now take the outline as we noted it under Argument, and expand it into a final letter.

THE LETTER ITSELF:

Before we show the final letter, let's repeat our first attempt:

From: T. Smith, QA
To: Mrs R. Jones, Branch Manager, Winchester

We are receiving a growing number of complaints about the cleanliness of your branch. Winchester branch is now top of the list in the "Action" table. As branch manager, you should realise that dirty and untidy premises are not consistent with the Society's image of friendly professionalism. I would ask you therefore to take immediate steps to ensure that the appearance of the branch gives no cause for future complaints.

10A Form for: Letter to branch manager, Winchester

1. **Aims** (operational objective)
   create friendly and business-like image to increase sales.

2. **Action** (desired effect of the communication)
   manager keep branch looking friendly and business-like.

3. **Author** (sender of the communication)
   Quality Assurance Manager. tribe = BBS/QA/HO. aim = correct
   problems affecting promotion of friendly/business-like image.

4. **Audience** (recipients of the communication)
   branch manager. tribe = BBS/Winchester branch/Hampshire.
   aim = sell products/promote friendly business-like image in
   Winchester.

5. **Affinity** (relationship between author and audience)
   teamwork = "Let's work together to project friendly business-
   like image." pleading = "Help". selling = "here's how".

6. **Angle** (point of view to be adopted)
   shared. author. audience.

7. **Argument (supporting reasoning)**
   intro.
       explain QA function.
       problem with your branch.
           look at attached complaints.
   need for corrective action.
       consider changing cleaners?
       need someone to check out appearance, cleanliness, pens,
         leaflets, flowers, teddy bear?
           have rota for it (eg Southampton)?
   report progress/problems.
       use same solution elsewhere?

8. **Appraisal** (checkpoint)
   OK.

9. **Articulation** (how the communication is expressed)
   informal. friendly.

10. **Appearance** (physical appearance of the communication)
    short letter. typewriter Courier. attach complaints.

Compare it with the following example:

From: Terry Smith, Manager, Quality Assurance
To: Robin Jones, Branch Manager, Winchester

As you may have read in the branch newsletters, the Society has set up a new department to monitor customer complaints received by the Chief Executive. As you know, he's especially keen on our friendly and business-like image.

As it happens, it seems that your branch is receiving more than its fair share of criticism about its appearance. (We have attached some copies so you can read them for yourself. "Disgusted from Alresford" is particularly vocal on the subject!) We know very well that you manage one of our busiest branches, but we all urgently need your help on this.

It may be that the cleaners are the problem, so you may care to show them the complaints. Or you may decide to give the job to another firm. We will leave that to you.

However, you might also like to borrow an idea from Alex in Southampton. Apparently, she has a rota system, whereby one of the staff is given the job of checking out the premises throughout the day to make sure everything is as it should be. The job includes not only removing litter, but also keeping display material up to date, making sure the pens work, buying flowers occasionally, or even having a teddy bear to keep the toddlers amused!

Please call Alex or me if you want to know more. In any event, do let me know how you get on. If it works in Winchester as well as it does in Southampton, I'm sure the chief exec will want to put out a memo to all branch managers so they can follow the example set by you and Alex.

The two letters are very different. But one of them is more likely to achieve our objective. The revised letter turned out to be rather longer than the original.

This was the result of adding a few ideas to make it more effective. However, this doesn't always happen. Sometimes the end result is much shorter because we discover we can throw away material we don't need.

This example gives an idea of the power of the 10A Technique. It helps us think clearly about certain things we might not otherwise consider, and how to create a persuasive argument. In the case above, this resulted in a completely different approach and a change of tone. This is much more easily handled before we start drafting. (One of the hardest things in writing is deleting what we've already written. Once we've composed a few paragraphs, we tend to use them, even when we know they're not quite right.)

Because we haven't yet covered the 10A Technique in detail, you might be wondering about some of the changes we made, and how we came to make them. This will all be explained in the rest of the book.

Meet the Fuddle Corporation

At this point, we'd like to introduce the 'Fuddle Corporation', an organisation that we have invented in order to provide a background to the various cases and examples we shall be discussing. The Fuddle Corporation is, of course, fictitious. Nevertheless, it is real in the sense that it is a composite of most of the organisations we have worked with over the years.

What products or services it offers is quite irrelevant. (In fact, we're not quite sure ourselves, and it's entirely possible that Fuddle employees don't know either.) The important characteristic of Fuddle is that it is run by a number of discrete departments or divisions, and is therefore prone to outbreaks of internal tribal warfare. From time to time, it also has skirmishes with customers and suppliers. This leads to a certain amount of confusion. You might recognise your own organisation immediately. In which case, you're going to feel quite at home.

Pinned to the wall in the office of the Director of Administration is an organisation chart looking like the one in Figure 1.3. There are similar charts in every other director's office, except that, in each case, their own department tends to occupy the prominent left-hand position instead of Admin. Also, the one in Personnel has recently been amended to show 'Human Resources' instead.

This, then, is the battleground. But first, before hostilities begin, we need to consider whether we should be writing at all. How do we decide whether we should meet, phone or write?

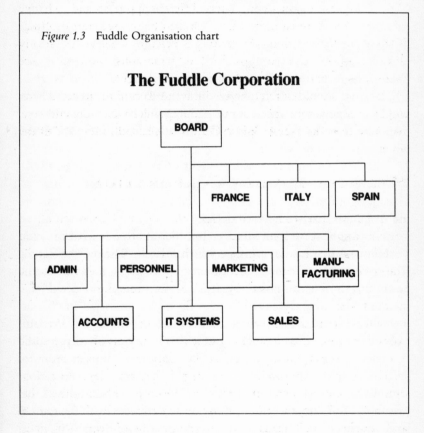

Figure 1.3 Fuddle Organisation chart

The Fuddle Corporation

2. Meet, Phone or Write?

One of the critical decisions to make when planning our message is whether we should meet, phone, or write to our audience. There will be occasions when meeting or phoning will be far more effective than a letter or a written report. On the other hand, there are times when only writing will do.

The 10A Technique is independent of the medium to be used. Whichever method we choose, the essential components of managing our message are identical, and it's only when we come to the Appraisal that we have to decide.

This might seem a bit strange, but the rationale behind the 10A Technique is that it's the message which matters. The most effective strategy is to plan the message, and then check which method should be employed to communicate it. It is a serious mistake to decide the medium first, and then try to make the communication fit. If our message is complex or important, it may be compromised as a result.

For example, if we decide to put across a very involved proposal in a telephone call, we may well have to omit key points in order to keep it simple. Alternatively, we could find ourselves repeating arguments several times because our listener cannot follow the reasoning. On the other hand, if we write a report which contains a large number of questions or conditional statements ('If it is Marketing's intention to . . . then we would recommend . . . or if Marketing has decided to . . . then we suggest that . . .' etc), this is a clear sign that we should have had a meeting with Marketing beforehand to clarify the situation.

During our workshops, the session on when to meet, phone or write provokes a great deal of discussion and disagreement. When we ask participants which medium they would use, the top-of-the-head response is normally 'we write when we can't phone, and phone when we can't meet'. But when we present them with some sample situations, they only arrive at a consensus after considerable debate, and sometimes not even then.

Two points emerge from all of this. Firstly, some types of situation are less than clear-cut. They are pregnant with both opportunities and dangers, and it is not always easy to see what we should do. Secondly, beyond the feeling that frequent contact is the way to build relationships and get things done, most of our participants cheerfully admit that they had never before given the problem a moment's thought! We therefore offer some basic guidelines on choosing the right medium, based upon the essential differences between meeting, phoning and writing.

Figure 2.1 shows a rough and ready 'Decision Matrix' which will serve as a quick guide to which medium to use. The table ignores instances when all three methods could be used, and concentrates on cases when one or two of them are appropriate. Bear in mind that a

---

Figure 2.1 Meet, Phone or Write? – Decision Matrix

	M	P	W
Long distance?		✓	✓
One-to-many?	✓		✓
One-to-very many?			✓
Show commitment?	✓	✓	
Seeking clarification?	✓	✓	
Discuss and explore?	✓	✓	
Urgent answer needed?	✓	✓	
Considered response needed?			✓
Complex argument?			✓
Visible evidence?	✓		✓
Audible/tangible evidence?	✓		
Language problems?			✓
Permanent record?			✓
Off-the-record?	✓	✓	

---

perfect fit may not be possible. A written report, for example, may need to be backed up with a meeting or phone call, and vice versa.

What happens when we meet?

Meetings are potentially demanding in terms of time and travel, and can be hard to arrange. Consequently, all attendees expect some benefit from the meeting – indeed, some may bring along their own agenda.

However, whether one-to-one, one-to-many, or many-to-many, participants can interact and provide feedback to each other. Meetings can therefore be very helpful if we need to explore a range of views (as in committee meetings), or to test the audience's understanding and agreement. We can also take the opportunity to have a closer look at the other participants, or 'check them out'. This works both ways – sales people like to use their interpersonal skills to generate confidence and put prospects at their ease. Equally, they can bring along a squadron of support people to demonstrate the depth of their resources (and field the hard questions).

There is, however, the danger that participants will 'perform' at meetings. Market research companies sometimes make the mistake of organising group discussions on a particular subject, only to find that one or two attendees use it as a personal platform: they take the opportunity to demonstrate their knowledge and experience and, of course, their speaking abilities. The others either resent this and disagree for the sake of it, or they follow the leader. Not very helpful when the client wants genuine unbiased opinions.

Finally, we believe that far too many people call meetings without questioning the need for them. This seems to be driven by a wish to socialise, or the feeling that position and status will be reinforced by personal contact – many managers like to be seen at the 'coal face'. Unfortunately, this encourages the culture that 'meetings are the way we do business around here', and many work-hours are lost as a result.

Meetings are good in situations when:

- **We want to show commitment or engagement** – The fact that we have taken the trouble to come shows we care. (This is also true of the audience: they have come with expectations which we must meet.)
- **We need an urgent decision**
- **We have to involve a number of people in a discussion and reach conclusions within a reasonable time frame** – Especially when we need visible support from our experts, or when we are facing several decision-makers.
- **The argument is complex, with many conditional effects** – That is, when the development of the argument or proposition depends upon reaction from the audience
- **We need to use visible or tangible material to support the argument**
- **We (or the audience) want something to be off the record**

WHAT HAPPENS WHEN WE PHONE?

Talking on the phone gives us some of the advantages of meeting. We can interact to a certain extent with our audience, but we do not have visual feedback. How, for instance, do we interpret a sudden silence at the other end of the line? Is our audience frowning, nodding, or speaking with their hand over the mouthpiece to someone else? Or perhaps they are bending down to retrieve the pen they just dropped. Maybe our 'off-the-record' discussion is being interrupted while they're changing the tape!

For the caller, phone calls are a quick and convenient way of making contact. However, for the audience, they are often unsolicited, and may well be intrusive. These two factors present us with the biggest problems.

Many managers are inundated with phone calls precisely because the medium offers a quick and cheap way of attracting their attention. Our audience may decide to be 'out' or 'at a meeting' if they are busy. Many senior managers employ someone to 'guard the gate', and we may well find ourselves presenting our credentials to the secretary and giving them a rehearsal of our message before we are connected.

Most importantly, even if we're lucky and they do pick up the phone, our audience can hang up whenever they choose. Especially if they don't like what they are hearing.

In some situations, we can live with these problems. Telesales reps, for example, use the phone extensively when 'prospecting' for new clients. They use special scripts, and play a 'numbers game', knowing that a large number of calls attempted will result in a useful proportion of contacts made. However, this strategy is inappropriate when it's a question of reaching a key individual on an important matter.

The most common mistake with phoning is trying to achieve too much, either by asking for detailed information which the audience does not have to hand, or expecting a quick decision on a proposal supported by an extensive argument. In each case, the audience needs time, either to collect information or to consider the argument. A professional sales representative is aware of this, and will hesitate to ask for an order on the phone, preferring to go for something which the audience can easily agree to there and then, such as an appointment to meet.

Phone calls can be used when:

- **It's urgent** – Phone calls travel only slightly slower than the speed of light.
- **We can't meet because distance is a problem** – Don't forget time zones, of course. When we were working for an American company, phone calls used to ruin anything arranged for our Friday evenings.
- **It's one-to-one** – Conference calls, in our experience, are mostly taken up with 'Who's that speaking now?' or 'Are *you* still there, Alex?'
- **We can express our argument in words without referring to visual evidence**

- **The reason for the call can be simply and persuasively expressed within a few seconds** – Once the audience is 'hooked', we can take more time with the argument. If we can't hook them quickly, we'll never get to the argument.
- **The audience will understand** – A simple point, but increasingly important in the context of dealing with others in the EC. Any linguist will tell us that reading and writing a foreign language is a hundred times easier than having to listen to it and speak it on the phone.

WHAT HAPPENS WHEN WE WRITE?

We once heard a speaker at a computer conference announce that he had invented a simple, effective and inexpensive communications medium. The process began with chopping down trees and mashing them into a wet pulp. The pulp could be flattened and, when dry, cut into flexible discrete modules, available in different sizes. The user could encode his message manually or mechanically on one or more of these modules. The modules could then be reproduced in unlimited quantities and physically transmitted to any geographical location. They could be read by the recipient(s) without any special decoding equipment. They could be stored offline almost indefinitely without noticeable degradation, could be quickly retrieved at any time, and would not take up any disk space whatsoever. He was convinced the medium had a great future. We agree. When used properly, paper can have considerable advantages.

We write when:

- **We need to address a number of people at the same time**
- **The argument or explanation is complex, or when visual aids and supporting material are needed** – Writing gives the author time to plan the argument, and the audience time to think and review it.
- **We don't feel we can trust our own interpersonal skills** –

Some of us can write reasonably articulately, but fear we will lapse into incoherence in a personal confrontation. This is very common when making proposals or complaints to a high level audience.

- **We want a considered response** – There are times when we suspect that what we want to say will be rejected out of hand at a meeting or on the phone. We need the audience to think before they adopt a position from which they will find it hard to back down.
- **An accurate and permanent record is required**
- **When we want to slow a transaction down**
- **It's the only way!** – There is little point banging on the door of Number 10 (or the MD's office, for that matter) to deliver our thoughts on how we think things might be better organised.

SECOND THOUGHTS

Sometimes, a snap judgement on whether to meet, phone or write seems obviously correct, but a moment's concentration will point to a better solution, or to the realisation that a combination of methods will be necessary.

> **The MD of Fuddle has asked the Marketing Director to find out from the regional sales managers why sales of some products are not meeting targets.**

The Marketing Director knows that the final report to the MD must be in written form. However, when it comes to collecting the information for the report, things are not quite so clear. His decision is to go for a big meeting, because that's his usual way of doing things. But we know that this could well result in performances and coordinated 'axe-grinding'. On the other hand, a series of individual meetings could take time to arrange, so perhaps he should phone each of the sales managers separately for their comments.

It is, however, quite probable that the reasons for poor sales will be complex and controversial, and therefore he might need to have the findings on record. In addition, most people take more care with facts and accusations when committing themselves in writing. He could phone each of them in turn, asking for a written report.

Probably the best solution would be to send a written memo requesting a report. The memo would be addressed to the sales managers *as a group,* thus letting each of them know that they are not being singled out for special attention. Hopefully, this might avoid defensive postures and 'pre–emptive retaliation'. It also has the benefit of being able to prove he did ask, even if they don't reply!

One of the Fuddle sales reps has just taken a large order from his most important customer. Now he discovers that the product has been discontinued. He would like the customer to order an alternative.

The correct course would be to go and see the client. Only in this way can he tell him the bad news, and begin to sell him an alternative. But would he call unannounced? No, he would call to make an appointment. What would he give as the reason for the visit? If he actually explained the full reason, he would run the risk of having to hold the conversation on the phone there and then, possibly resulting in outright rejection. He has no way of preventing the customer hanging up in disgust. The only sure way is to ask to meet to talk over some undefined problem which is 'a bit too involved to handle on the phone', or alternatively to arrive at a time when he's sure the client will be there and will see him.

The IT Manager has just made a job offer to a very promising candidate. Now he has to tell her that recruitment has just been frozen.

The IT manager just shrugs his shoulders and drops her a line to formally withdraw the verbal offer. The letter puts it on the record, but he might have seen the value of an apologetic phone call first to preserve the relationship. After all, the freeze may not last forever. (On our workshops, we have occasionally had students – obviously destined for greater things – who suggest a more Machiavellian tactic. They would phone her, asking her to send in her acceptance right away, backdated before the date of the freeze!)

The Purchasing Manager has just received a note from Accounts, pointing out that there are discrepancies in a number of invoices presented by one of Fuddle's main suppliers over the last nine months. (Copies are enclosed which apparently show overcharging.) He did not spot these when he passed them for payment.

The Purchasing Manager dictates a stiffish letter to the supplier, asking for an explanation. This is not a good idea. The supplier must now defend his position formally, and the Purchasing Manager himself will have some embarrassing questions to answer if the correspondence has to escalate.

Phone calls all round, we think, and the Purchasing Manager will have to trust that the supplier agrees to rectify the mistakes. Only in this way can everybody stay 'off the hook' and carry on doing business with each other.

WHO DECIDES?

If we initiate the contact, we are comparatively free to choose the most effective medium ourselves. But what should we do if we are specifically requested to meet, phone or write? It is our message that we are managing, and it's our responsibility to give it our best shot. Even if we have to attend a meeting, then we can still back it up with a written report or with handouts if our message requires it. Similarly, if we are expected to produce a written report, we can still ask for a meeting to present it, or make a phone call to warn of its arrival and its conclusions if we think it's necessary.

A common problem arises when we receive a sudden phone call asking for information which we were planning to put in a written report. We have to respond in some way, but we risk being sidetracked into a complicated discussion which is difficult to conduct orally. This often happens when the caller begins by asking the wrong question:

Quality Manager:	I need a quick report on the failure of the Mark IV. What happened?
Engineering Manager:	The A-bracket broke.
Quality Manager:	I know that! Why did it break?
Engineering Manager:	There were a number of reasons.
Quality Manager:	Such as?
Engineering Manager:	Well, for a start, the operator was running the machine outside design specifications ...
Quality Manager:	So it's down to operator negligence?
Engineering Manager:	It's not as easy as that. There were a number of other factors ...
Quality Manager:	Oh?
Engineering Manager:	We think the original design tolerances might be too wide ...
Quality Manager:	Who's 'we'?
Engineering Manager:	Well, I do. And Fred Zimowski.
Quality Manager:	Fred who?

And so on . . .

The caller – the Quality Manager – is running the conversation, and the Engineering Manager is having difficulty organising and presenting the evidence and conclusions. If the Quality Manager has the patience, he may eventually find out what happened. More likely, after a few circular references ('But I thought I explained that just now . . .'), he will give up the struggle and hang up, convinced that the Engineering Manager is incompetent.

In this situation, it is better to cut it short with a warning (explicit or implied) that the subject is too complex to handle on the phone. Give a brief statement of the conclusions, and a promise to provide a full report:

Quality Manager:	I need a quick report on the failure of the Mark IV. What happened?
Engineering Manager:	I've had a number of senior engineers examine the machine, and we found that there were a number of factors involved. The bottom line is that we need to make two design changes which will solve the problem. I'm preparing a detailed report for you, with some photos we took of the damaged part. You should get it tomorrow.
Quality Manager:	OK, thanks.

The caller now has the answer to the question he probably meant to ask in the first place: 'Have you investigated and found a solution?' If he really wants to know exactly what happened, then he will understand that it's going to take some time for the Engineering Manager to explain it on the phone, and that he needs to see some photos. He'll probably wait for the report.

The opposite type of sidetrack is when we want a meeting or a phone conversation, but the minder has the chain on the door:

Office Manager:	I need to speak to the Personnel Manager please.
Secretary:	He's very busy just at the moment. Can I ask what it's about?
Office Manager:	I'd rather not say.
Secretary:	I can't disturb him without telling him what it's about.
Office Manager:	I'd really rather not say.
Secretary:	Perhaps you could drop him a line?
Office Manager:	Not really. I have to speak to him.
Secretary:	Well, I can't put you through unless you tell me what it's all about.

Office Manager: All right then. Three of the girls want to
make a complaint about sexual
harassment by one of the senior
managers ...
Secretary: Gosh! Really? Which one?

The rest of the conversation (and the consequences) we'll leave to
your imagination!

The Office Manager should have refused to play the game:

Office Manager: I need to speak to the Personnel Manager
please.
Secretary: He's very busy just at the moment. Can I
ask what it's about?
Office Manager: It's a very important and confidential
matter, and I know he would want to hear
about it immediately.
Secretary: All right. Hang on ...

Nothing particularly original here. Telephone sales people use
this ploy all the time, but it works. The trick is to sow a seed of
doubt, and to suggest that the boss might be upset when he finds out
that he was prevented from taking the call.

Now it's time to turn to the 10A Technique itself. As we go
through the process, we can bear in mind the relative advantages and
pitfalls of meeting, phoning and writing. When we come to
Appraisal, we should have a clear idea of which medium (or
combinations of methods) our message requires.

SUMMARY

- Use the 10A Technique to plan the message first
- Let the message decide the medium
- Use a combination of methods if necessary, for instance
  - briefing notes for meetings
  - circulation of minutes of meetings
  - presentations to support written reports
  - a letter of confirmation following an important phone call
  - calls to follow up sales letters
- When specifically asked to meet or phone or write, do as asked, PLUS whatever you think necessary, for instance:
  - handouts and samples at presentations
  - a phone call to warn of an important report
  - a written report to support a meeting
- Avoid being dragged into expressing your argument in an unsuitable medium, for instance:
  - trying to explain a complex report orally
  - attempting an interview by letter
  - putting an off-the-record matter in writing!

3. Aims

The 10A Technique helps construct a message which is consistent with some overall objective. Identifying our aims, therefore, is the single most important exercise in the planning of our communication. That's why it's top of the list. If we fail to get our Aims right, our message will fail too.

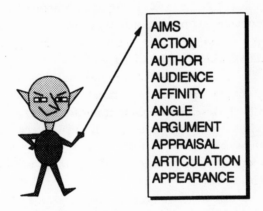

AIMS
ACTION
AUTHOR
AUDIENCE
AFFINITY
ANGLE
ARGUMENT
APPRAISAL
ARTICULATION
APPEARANCE

Jim has a story about how he got his Aims wrong:

I was once a young and keen computer manager in an insurance company.

One of the things an insurance company has to do is assess the value of its insurance contracts. Traditionally, this had been done by a host of actuaries using complicated statistical techniques.

To me, this seemed extremely labour-intensive. After I had been there a few months, I wrote a report to the Chief Actuary announcing that I had thought of a way of reducing the number of actuaries he needed. I described how the new computer system could calculate automatically the value of each and every contract.

The Chief Actuary summoned me to his office. He handed the report back to me, and said: 'Young man. While I subscribe to the principle of reducing costs, I do not accept that dismissing my actuaries is an objective. And I am confident that the General Manager – as an actuary himself – will share my view. However, I warn you that neither of us has any reservations about releasing computer staff.'

This chapter explores Aims, making us ask: 'What are we trying to achieve?' (**Note:** This is not the same as: 'What do we expect the communication to achieve?' This is what we call the Action, and we shall deal with that in the next chapter. Aims makes us think about where we're trying to go: Action is about how we get there.)

WHY AIMS ARE IMPORTANT

We need to identify our aims for a number of reasons. Firstly, we need to establish a reference point for our message. As we go through the 10A Technique, it is quite normal to change our mind about the steps involved in achieving our objectives, about our Audience, about the way to motivate them, about various details in our Argument, and even who the Author should be! When presented with options in this way, we need an anchor for the whole process. Aims and Action provide just that. The sole criterion for the message is whether it will result in the Action we have specified for it. And the Action will be judged by whether it will contribute to our Aims.

Secondly, the process of establishing aims will help us find an objective which our audience can share. This will be the basis of our relationship with them, and will point to the various ways in which we can motivate them and secure their cooperation.

Finally, there will be times when we ourselves cannot see the way forward. We can describe the problem, but not the solution. Our audience may be able to help if they understand what it is that we're trying to achieve.

EXPRESSING AIMS

When we plan our message, we normally have some idea of our objective. Unfortunately, many communications fail because we do not *express* it, or we express an aim which the audience finds irrelevant or threatening:

From: Training Manager
To: Sales Director

We have a number of vacancies on the ST/09 module scheduled for week 15. I will have to cancel this course if it is undersubscribed. I would appreciate it, therefore, if you could let me have a list of your nominations as soon as possible.

What will the Sales Director's Goblin say?

**"What on earth is ST/09?
Cancel the course?
Heaven forfend! Our heart will
bleed . . ."**

The Fuddle Training Manager forgot to express an overall objective to which the Sales Director could subscribe. His use of tribal jargon (ST/09 module) gives no clue what the course is about. Consequently, the Sales Director sees no relevance to him. The Training Manager's implied aim was to avoid having to cancel the course, so the memo asks for a list of nominations for it. He receives little sympathy from the Sales Director who probably has problems of his own to worry about.

In this simple case, there were no fatalities. The Training Manager will just have to try again. But sometimes the consequences of this elementary error can be serious, as Jim nearly discovered in the story at the beginning of the chapter.

STRUCTURING OBJECTIVES

When thinking about aims, we tend to think first about our personal and departmental responsibilities and accountabilities. These, however, are only a starting point. When dealing with other departments or higher levels of management, we need to consider the broader picture as seen by our audience. When we do this, we tend to find ourselves presented with a number of possibilities, often in some sort of hierarchy.

Let's look at an everyday case. We want to sell our house. Looking at the situation as a whole, we could envisage a structure of aims in which each item can be seen as an 'objective', when seen from below, or a 'means', when viewed from above (Figure 3.1).

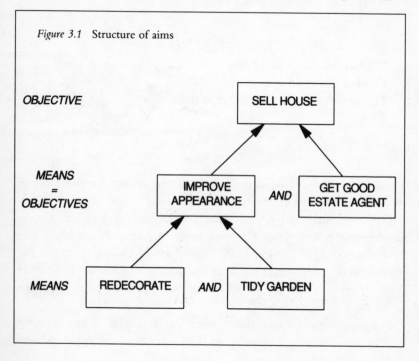

Figure 3.1 Structure of aims

In this case, our ultimate goal is selling the house for a good price. This objective could be satisfied by two contributing means, improving its appearance and getting a good estate agent. Now, taking improving the appearance of the property as an objective, we can see that the contributing means are to redecorate the house and tidy up the garden.

If we are wondering just who is going to do the redecorating, then we can use at least some of this structure of objectives to get assistance. We have four choices. We can persuade our teenage offspring to do it; or our partner; or we can do it ourselves; or we can call a decorator. If we now map their objectives onto ours, we can see our options more clearly (Figure 3.2).

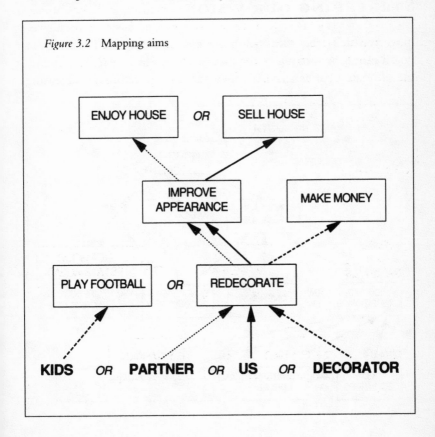

Figure 3.2 Mapping aims

Unfortunately the kids only want to play football, and they see this as incompatible with the task of redecorating. Next, we have a problem with our partner who simply wants to stay in the house and enjoy living in it. Though our partner doesn't want to sell it, we can point out that improving the appearance and redecorating will also contribute to their own long-term goal. So our partner may pick up a paint brush rather than entrust the task to our own dubious skills.

Finally, when the professional decorator calls, it's not much good talking about selling the house or even improving its appearance. They might nod in sympathy, but they're really only in it for the money.

STRETCHING OUR VISION

If we transport this idea into a business context, the Fuddle main board might be looking at the picture shown in Figure 3.3. Taking the ultimate goal as survival, they can see the means as increasing

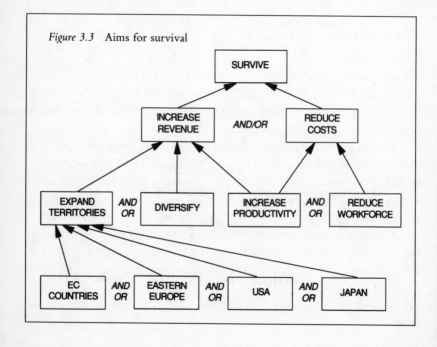

Figure 3.3   Aims for survival

revenue and/or reducing costs. The objective of increasing revenue can be met by expanding territories and/or diversifying. In turn, the objective of expanding territories can be met by getting into any combination of EC countries, Eastern Europe, USA or Japan.

If we want to take part in a strategic discussion of this kind, we need to see the same picture that they're scratching their heads over. This means opening up our own perspective to take in the broader view. If we think it would be a great move to expand into Poland, for instance, we must be able to relate our idea to the board's perception of objectives. It's not a good plan to leave it to them to make the connection.

In this case, we should also recognise that 'territorial expansion' might be just one option the board directors are chewing over in the fight for survival. We may have competition from someone who thinks our priority should be diversification. As we shall see later under Appraisal, our proposition will have more authority if we can demonstrate that we are aware of options and alternatives.

RELATING OBJECTIVES

As we saw with the house, it is useful to be able to relate objectives and means to each other. If we assume that the Fuddle main board has decided to have a look at expanding into Poland, we could imagine a structure of aims as in Figure 3.4:

To achieve the goal, we need to build a distribution capability and customise our products for the Polish market. When looking at distribution, we are faced with some options, setting up a subsidiary, acquiring an existing outlet, appointing a distributor, or trying to do it by mail order.

This schematic is reasonably self-contained. Anyone involved in the activities shown could be expected to appreciate the relationships. If we want the Legal department to look into registering a company in Poland, then we could demonstrate that we are all working towards the objective of opening up the Polish market.

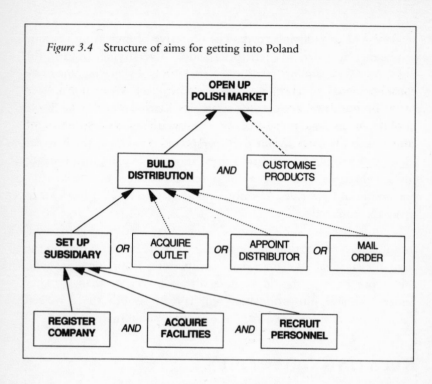

Figure 3.4 Structure of aims for getting into Poland

However, if the link is too remote, the objective is that much harder to describe convincingly. Supposing we want Personnel to investigate the recruitment of a Polish workforce: stating an objective of 'increasing revenue' for the company (from the earlier, higher-level picture) will sound somewhat bizarre. (Rather like the customer engineer who asks for a new company car in the interests of greater customer satisfaction.)

The schematic also shows up areas of potential conflict when we see that some objectives are mutually exclusive. If we're wondering who to approach in Personnel about the Polish recruitment problem, we had better not ask the person who – in the previous top level plan – has just been assigned the task of reducing headcount. Or, if we are convinced that setting up our own subsidiary is the way to go, we are likely to get into a tangle with someone else who happens to be busy sounding out potential distributors.

TRIBAL AIMS

When thinking laterally (and vertically) about aims, it's helpful to consider tribes and tribal aims. Other tribes' ultimate goal is always survival, but how they see themselves getting there will vary. Looking at the Fuddle Sales Tribe, Figure 3.5 shows a structure of aims which the Sales Director should recognise.

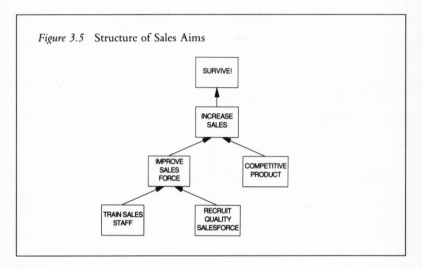

Figure 3.5 Structure of Sales Aims

Their means of survival is increased sales. To achieve this, they need an effective sales force and a competitive product. (No doubt they need a few other things like good pricing, promotion, a strong support infrastructure etc, but let's keep it simple for the moment.) There are two obvious ways of improving the sales force – training existing staff and recruitment.

To take it a stage further, tribal members will also have personal aims, again, all designed to help each of them survive. Although our Fuddle Training Manager belongs to: (a) the Fuddle Tribe; (b) the Human Resources Tribe; and (c) the Training Tribe, he also has a personal aim. His way of ensuring survival is to create for himself the reputation as 'The Best Training Manager Fuddle Ever Had And Could Not Possibly Do Without.'

At the moment, he has the problem of the course on week 15 that no one wants to go on. He might have picked up a pen and drawn the following schematic (Figure 3.6) to see how his own objectives could be mapped on to the Sales Director's.

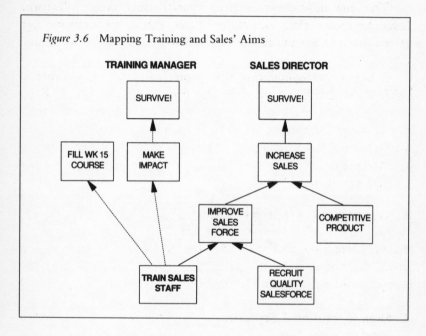

Figure 3.6   Mapping Training and Sales' Aims

While the Training Manager is interested in making a personal impact and filling the course on week 15, he can see that getting sales personnel on the course is the way to achieve both. But where does this fit with the Sales Director's aims? The course is a way to improve the sales force, and thereby increase sales. Thus he might have written a rather different memo:

From: Training Manager
To: Sales Director

As you may know, we are running a series of training courses in order to improve the effectiveness of our sales force. You will be pleased to hear that there are still some vacancies on the course scheduled for week 15. If you will let me have a list of your nominations, I will take care of the bookings for you.

This time, he has expressed an operational objective which the Sales Director could be expected to share: 'to improve the effectiveness of our sales force'. Who knows? He might have some takers.

If Jim at the beginning of the chapter had taken the trouble to think about the chief actuary and his tribe, he would have realised that one of his audience's most important aims would be to ensure that he did not lose any of the army of actuaries he'd built up over the years. Jim might have done better to point out how the new system would give the actuaries the freedom to have a go at some more exciting calculations.

USING THE 10A FORM

At this starting point on the 10A Form, all we have to do is enter a brief description of the aims we have identified for the communication. For example:

1. Aims (operational objective)
   effective sales force.

A little later, we shall be making similar notes about aims under both Author and Audience, and comparing the three entries will suggest ways of motivating our Audience.

SUMMARY

- Identify the reason for the communication
- Think about the 'big picture'
- Try to structure operational objectives into a hierarchy
- Keep in mind where the Aims fit
- Note areas of possible conflict

4. Action

Now we have some idea of our Aims, it is time to consider how we go about achieving them. The Action is the intended effect of a communication, and it must in some way contribute to the Aim. The rules are simple: the Action should support the Aim, and not be irrelevant to it, or conflict with it. It must also be clearly understood by the Audience.

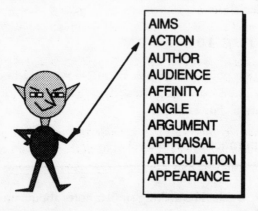

AIMS
ACTION
AUTHOR
AUDIENCE
AFFINITY
ANGLE
ARGUMENT
APPRAISAL
ARTICULATION
APPEARANCE

The following true tale tells what happened when an Author failed to take care when expressing an Action.

A colleague of ours was manager in the Customer Engineering Department. One day, it was drawn to his notice that, due to a printing error, some service contracts had been sent out in the last year with a page missing. The text in question listed some important exclusions and, without this page in the signed agreement, the company would be liable for a variety of claims which could cost them a very great deal of money.

Nobody knew how many faulty documents had been issued, but since there were many thousands of contracts on the books, the consequences could be serious.

Before any action could be taken, however, they needed to know the extent of the problem. The manager therefore decided to have someone run quickly through the files to check.

He wrote an urgent memo to one of his supervisors which briefly explained the situation, and that only contracts in the preceding twelve months might be affected. He ended the memo with the words 'please let me have details of each case.'

Two days passed. He called the supervisor and was assured that the task was in hand. Another two days went by, so he decided to call round in person.

To his amazement, he found a small brigade of clerks and office temps seated around a large table. They were laboriously copying down details from piles of contracts.

The manager was very uneasy: 'I had no idea there would be this many faulty ones.'

'There aren't,' the supervisor assured him. 'We've only come across fifteen so far.'

The manager frowned: 'So what on earth are all these people doing?'

'They are taking down particulars of all the last year's contracts. You asked for details of each case,' the supervisor reminded him. 'Didn't you?'

The need to express the Action clearly should be obvious, but the very idea of separating the Action from the Aim has a number of advantages too. For a start, it makes us think positively about what we actually want to happen as a result of the communication.

Let's say we're planning a mailshot to customers, telling them about price reductions on certain products. The Aim would be to sell the products. The Action could be for customers to phone and speak to sales staff. When writing the mailshot, we should specifically ask for this, and this would suggest to us that we find ways of making it easy to do, such as a toll-free call to a special number constantly manned.

Secondly, when we plan a communication, we sometimes start with the Action, instead of the Aim. A reminder sent to an important customer to chase up an overdue account would have an Action of requiring the customer to send a cheque. The discipline of the 10A Technique, however, suggests that we find an Aim as well. This has the effect of obliging us to face the real problem. It could be to persuade this customer to pay within 30 days in future, in which case a personal visit from our own Sales Director will have more impact than a standard reminder which will never get further than their Accounts Payable clerk. If we have several such delinquents, the Aim might become to reduce payment arrears from large customers. We might then point out to the Sales Director the potential benefit of a special deal for 'valued customers' involving a small discount in return for early payment. In both cases, we are being creative and adding-value to our existence.

The process is also self-checking. If we find we have put down an Action which is the same as our Aim, this is a little red flag to warn us we have got one or the other wrong. We may be concerned about our office staff's habitual lateness, for instance, and we begin to draft a memo. We could find that we have 'staff to arrive punctually at the office in future' as both the Aim and the Action. Foul! We must step back and ask ourselves what our aim really is.

This can be very illuminating. A revised Aim of ensuring that the office runs efficiently will force us to question whether the Action of getting staff to arrive punctually at the office in future really will contribute to it. In other words, is staff lateness in the morning a problem or not? It could be that it isn't, and we may well realise that our people often work late of their own accord to get the job done. So we scrap the memo, and by so doing we avoid upsetting our conscientious staff with a note that they will see as both fussy and ungrateful – one which may also encourage them to be fastidious clock-watchers.

COMMON ERRORS WITH ACTION

The most frequent and time-consuming mistake is a simple failure to state what is wanted:

From: Admin Director
To: Printing Services Manager

At the board meeting yesterday, the Marketing Director was complaining that sales brochures have been out of stock for months. I said I would drop you a note about it.

"Oh goody . . ."

From: Printing Services Manager
To: Admin Director

Thank you.

This would have the Admin Director tearing his hair out, but whose fault was it? A variation on this is the ambiguous Action:

From: Admin Director
To: Printing Services Manager

At the board meeting yesterday, the Marketing Director was complaining that sales brochures have been out of stock for months. Is this true?

"Go on. Tell him!"

From: Printing Services Manager
To: Admin Director

I don't know. I wasn't there.

Even top management can unwittingly cause similar fun and games:

From: the Chairman
To: Marketing Director

I heard on the golf-course that our biggest competitor has
just signed large contracts with three water companies.
May I have your comments, please.

How is the Marketing Director to guess what may be wanted? The
problem is that the memo has two possible and conflicting
interpretations:

Either:

I heard on the golf-course that our biggest competitor has
just signed large contracts with three water companies.
How did we manage to lose out on these opportunities?

Or:

I heard on the golf-course that our biggest competitor has
just signed large contracts with three water companies. I
think this could be a good market for us too. Don't you agree?

The expected responses will be entirely different in each case, and
to guess at one or the other will risk embarrassment, to say the least.
After numerous calls to the Chairman's office at Headquarters (and
to the other one he always seems to have in the City) the Sales
Director will typically find that the Chairman is unavailable for
clarification. A quick check with the MD probably won't help much
either. Not good use of company resources!

The golden rule is *be explicit!*

TYPES OF ACTION

We can lay down another minefield for ourselves by not thinking clearly about the type of action required. For some reason, we tend to assume that our audience will know without prompting. In fact, there are really only four main types of action. Our communication can request or provide:

- Facts
- Interpretations
- Recommendations
- Executive action

Let's take a simple illustration:

From: the Managing Director
To: Administration Director

During fire alarm practice on Wednesday last, a number of personnel failed to go to the assembly area. Can you please tell me how many stayed in their offices, and why? This is a very serious matter, and I would like your suggestions on how we can ensure that everybody vacates the building in future. Meanwhile, please circulate a copy of fire safety procedures to all departmental managers.

This memo contains examples of requests for all four types of action:

- **Facts:** Can you please tell me how many stayed in their offices . . .?
- **Interpretation:** . . . and why?
- **Recommendations:** . . . I would like your suggestions on how we can ensure that everybody vacates the building in future.
- **Executive action:** . . . please circulate a copy of fire safety procedures to all departmental managers.

Each of these types of action implies a different level of capability and responsibility. Only the departments concerned would know how many of their own staff stayed at their desks, and what the reasons were in each case, so the Admin Director would have to find out from them.

However, the MD is not especially interested in why Alex, or Sandy, or Steve, or Chris failed to go to the assembly area, so the Admin Director would have the responsibility of finding meaningful patterns in their answers (interpretation). When it comes to making recommendations, he will probably need the assistance of a safety expert. Finally, it will be his own responsibility (and within his capability) to send out copies of fire safety procedures.

PROBLEMS WITH TYPES OF ACTION

The memo just quoted is explicit about what is wanted in terms of action, and the Admin Director should be in no doubt about what he has to do. However, we often see examples of what can go wrong when this is not spelled out:

From: Admin Director
To: Maintenance Manager

Sales are complaining that the lift broke down again on Thursday, this time with an important customer inside. Unfortunately, the gentleman suffers from claustrophobia and was too overcome to attend the presentation. Could you look into this, as I expect Sales will bring it up with the MD.

This could elicit the response:

From: Maintenance Manager
To: Admin Director

Please inform the MD that there is an intermittent short circuit in the switchgear. This causes the circuit-breaker to trip.

It's not our Admin Director's day, is it? He wanted the lift fixed but all he got was facts. Nevertheless, whose fault was it? This sort of sin of omission is unhappily all too frequent when we are complaining about something. We describe quite graphically what happened, and what the consequences were, but we leave out the all-important sentence: 'Since this is your responsibility, I want to know what went wrong, and what is being done to prevent it happening again.'

The failure to be explicit can also result in executive action when only opinions are needed.

From: Credit Control
To: Legal

The Controller has asked me to pass on to you some correspondence with ICI about an overdue invoice. Their last letter puts their position on why they are refusing to pay. We dispute the facts, of course.

From: Legal
To: Credit Control

I have reviewed the correspondence and would advise you that I have today applied for a winding-up order against the customer.

So far, we have laid the blame for these lapses at the door of the author. However, in the real world, we have to take some responsibility for our actions as audience too. If we receive a request, and we are in real doubt as to what is being asked for, it isn't an option to 'play games' or ignore it on the grounds that it was poorly expressed. If we really don't know what is expected of us, we must ask. There are no prizes for guessing.

COMMUNICATIONS ROADMAP

We have been discussing simple situations in order to make the points clearly. When taking our Aims and wondering what Actions we need to achieve them, we might have to perform a complicated task which must be broken down into separate steps. Each step might require one or more communications, and each communication will then have its own Action.

To take a straightforward example from selling, a pensions salesman planning his next round of prospecting might have an Aim of making a good living. One of the contributing means could be to sell some pensions. In practice, he would never construct an initial communication to a prospective customer which had this as the Action. (It would be too ambitious, and there are regulations which prevent it anyway.) He has to break the aim of selling some pensions down into these steps:

1. **Make a phone call in order to obtain an appointment**
2. **Meet with the prospect in order to collect information on prospect's financial arrangements and agree his or her objectives**
3. **At a later meeting, present his proposals and sell the pension**

This is a standard routine for selling pensions. In a wider business context, we have to give the same kind of thought as to how an overall Aim is to be achieved. We will return to the sales training issue in the Fuddle Corporation to illustrate this point.

The Sales Director was sufficiently persuaded by the Training Manager's second memo that he sent a number of his people on the week 15 course. Unfortunately, the sales people were not impressed. Ever since, the Sales Director has been hearing adverse comments, ranging from 'It was not entirely suited to my needs', through 'A waste of time', to 'Whose brilliant idea was that anyway?'

He accordingly asks his Sales Support Manager to investigate. She is to report on the effectiveness of the sales training courses currently being run. So far as the Sales Support Manager is concerned, the overall task is well-defined, but she can see that there will be a sequence of steps needed to complete it.

1. **Decide how to measure effectiveness** – She needs advice on this, but for the moment she can foresee the need to . . .
2. **Collect 'before and after' sales performance figures**
3. **Obtain comments from sales managers**
4. **Obtain comments from sales staff who have been on the course**
5. **Write the report**

All the steps involve communications, and the first four will each solicit actions in one form or another. She's not in a position to think about the Action of the final report, because at this stage, she doesn't know what the problem is, or whether there is a solution, let alone what the solution might be.

As a preliminary adjunct to the 10A Technique, she will find a 'Communications Roadmap' useful. She can set out each of the steps and its Action, along with the type of action, the taker of the action, and whether to meet, phone or write.

1. In order to measure effectiveness, she needs recommendations or suggestions on how to do this. But from whom? Personnel seem to have yardsticks for most things to do with people, so they might be able to help. This could be done with a phone call or a meeting.
2. The 'before and after' sales figures are facts. They will come from Accounts, and a quick memo or phone call asking for the figures in writing will do.
3. To complement the quantitative evidence from Accounts, she needs informed qualitative comment. This will consist of facts, interpretations and recommendations. These will come from the sales people who have been trained and their managers, and will be collected in meetings or phone calls.

Although this pre-plan may need changing as events unfold, the Sales Support Manager can now see at a glance the steps needed to get to the final report and where each of them fits in the overall task.

A Communications Roadmap will not be necessary in every case, nor will it always need writing down, but it can help break up an overall objective into smaller and more practical actions. It will also help slot the various jobs into a busy schedule, especially when travel is involved. (We may have one showing that we need to visit the same location to see different people for different reasons. The meetings can therefore be arranged for the same visit.)

USING THE 10A FORM

Under Action, we simply jot down what we expect the communication to achieve. For example, the memo to Accounts asking for the sales figures would have as its Aim and Action the following:

1. **Aims** (operational objective)
    report on effectiveness of sales training.
2. **Action** (desired effect of the communication)
    Accounts to provide sales figures.

In these last two chapters, we have covered the all-important Aims and Action. In the examples given, we have made assumptions about the author and audience involved in each case. In the next chapter, we will look at the implications of choosing a particular Author and Audience – as we shall see, this can lead to some unexpected conclusions.

SUMMARY

- List Actions which will contribute to the Aims
- Think about the type of action required
  - facts?
  - interpretations?
  - recommendations?
  - executive action?
- If you are doing the requesting, make sure recipient will understand what is wanted
  - If in doubt, spell it out!
- If you are responding, ask yourself if you are sure what is being asked for
  - If in doubt, ask!
- For complex tasks, set out the Actions in a Communications Roadmap.

5. Author and Audience

This chapter looks at Author and Audience, and it will help us decide who is to be involved in the Action on each side. Sometimes, we can get both wrong:

We know of a company where Marketing was permanently at loggerheads with the Financial Controller. The Marketing Director would openly refer to the Controller and his tribe as 'a band of bean-counters'. In turn, the Controller habitually described Marketing as 'a collection of cowboys'.

One day, a newly-appointed product marketing manager (who was innocently unaware of this long-standing antipathy) was preparing a business plan for a new product.

Rather than take the trouble to learn about mysterious things like Return on Investment and Return On Assets, he sends a note – off his own bat – to the Controller, asking for assistance.

The Controller doesn't recognise the name, but it's open season on Marketing people, and he eagerly sends across one of his top accountants armed with a calculator. After studying the draft plan for a while, the accountant finds what he's looking for. He asks the product manager what financial assumptions he has been making about indirect costs and overheads. The product manager assures him that he has been following Marketing's usual rules, and fishes out a number of earlier business plans to show him.

The accountant corrects the errors, and the product manager is left with a document which shows that his new product is no longer financially viable.

The accountant also dashes back to the Controller and gleefully reports that Marketing's business plans have never been worth the paper they were written on.

The subsequent post mortem between the Marketing Director and his product manager could be heard all over the building.

Moral? If you need swimming lessons, don't ask a shark! Or if you do, try not to look like its lunch.

AUTHOR

Our definition of Author is 'the person(s) or entity which the Audience sees as the agency behind the communication'. We must never forget that it's the Audience's perception which matters. Thus the apparent Author may or may not be the individual who actually composes the communication.

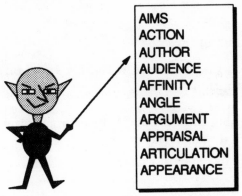

AIMS
ACTION
AUTHOR
AUDIENCE
AFFINITY
ANGLE
ARGUMENT
APPRAISAL
ARTICULATION
APPEARANCE

WHOSE MESSAGE IS IT ANYWAY?

In practice, it's surprising how seldom we're speaking just for ourselves as individuals. More frequently, we're acting on behalf of our department or organisation, or doing a bit of 'ghost-writing' for our manager. If you doubt this, you might care to check your own outgoing correspondence file. Ignore how the documents are actually signed, just look at a few of the personal pronouns. When you used 'I', did you really mean 'we'? And wherever you used 'we', just who did you have in mind?

We should take care in such situations, since our Audience is not likely to be adept at mind-reading. If we really have impressive credentials, we ought to make them work for us. Otherwise, we are abusing our responsibility towards our constituents.

In fact, the correct choice of Author can go a long way towards convincing the audience of our message. Our argument will be more readily accepted if there is a long-standing relationship built upon trust and confidence, and if the author has acknowledged expertise, integrity, and a reputation for being right. If we do not enjoy this credibility ourselves, then it's worth considering delegating authorship to someone who does.

Let's assume that one of the economists in the Controller's department thinks he ought to warn the MD about the possibility of an imminent rise in interest rates:

From: A. Jones
To: The Managing Director

I thought you may be interested in my views on the current economic situation ...

The MD probably doesn't know 'A. Jones' from Adam. Why should he bother with the note? The writer would have done better to send it over his director's name:

From: The Controller
To: The Managing Director

The attached briefing note summarises my department's views on the current economic situation ...

The MD will now read it simply because of the apparent Author. However, if 'A. Jones' happened to be the recognised authority on economic matters in the company, the following would be even more effective:

From: The Controller
To: The Managing Director

The attached briefing note was put together by Alex Jones, our senior financial analyst. It summarises my department's views on the current economic situation.

Regardless of who actually wrote the words, the MD will know (a) that the paper contains the views of somebody whose opinions have authority, (b) that it has the full backing of the Controller and his tribe, and (c) that he'd better read it and take note.

OVERSTATING CREDENTIALS

Overstating our credentials is, of course, just as bad as selling ourselves short. We're speaking for others when we're really on our own. This is not so much a deliberate attempt to deceive, but a spontaneous bid to strengthen our case. This can happen when we unconsciously indulge in the use of the Thatcheresque 'we':

From: Training Manager
To: Sales Support Manager

As you know, we have made tremendous efforts to put together a sales training course, and unfortunately this has consumed most of our budget. Since we all agree that the courses are very effective, everybody thinks it would be appropriate for you to make a financial contribution.

"Who is *we* exactly?"

"And who is *everybody*?"

If the Training Manager really did have the full backing of his boss (the Personnel Director), the MD, and all the other directors, he should have said so. Otherwise, he may as well have been frank and simply enquired whether some cash might be available to help him out.

We should never claim that we're speaking for others unless we're totally sure we are. This might mean having to pass around drafts and agreeing them with our 'constituents' before the final copy is sent. We should be honest if there are small areas of difference, since any hint of a cover-up will cast doubt on the credibility of our whole case. The extent of our backing should then be made clear in the text, and by copying in the names and titles of our supporters.

Another reason for testing the water first is that others may feel even more strongly than we do, and they might present us with additional arguments we hadn't previously thought of. This can only provide us with a stronger case.

NAME-DROPPING

While it is essential to make clear the extent of our support, we should be careful about name-dropping. Some of us like to mention influential people when we're making a case. Their endorsement can help, but one man's 'brilliant strategist' is another man's 'crooked numbskull'. The question to ask is whether the audience worships the same idol, or do they see feet of clay?

One manager we knew used to quote the opinions of the MD in order to lend weight to his messages. Whatever the subject, the MD had a view on it and, of course, it was always identical to the manager's. 'Gus feels we ought to be holding more sales seminars, and I agree with him . . .'. Or 'We ought to be looking at the education market, and I happen to know this is close to Gus's heart too . . .'.

One result was that he quickly came to be known as Gus's dummy. During meetings, his listeners – with straight faces – took to asking him questions like: 'Does Gus think this might be a good time for a coffee-break?' The other was that many of his ideas, whatever their merits, were dismissed out of hand. As it happened, most of his audiences had suffered in one way or another from something that Gus had said or done, so Gus's opinions weren't exactly popular with them.

COMPANY IMAGE

One particular circumstance which requires careful thought about the Author's credentials is when we're representing our organisation in dealings with customers. If our company is of any size, it probably has a corporate image that it wants to foster, and this is usually in the firm grip of an advertising agency. However, each of us has the opportunity and responsibility to present our organisation's credentials in sales proposals, presentations, and in day-to-day contact with customers and prospects. From observation, some make a better job of this than others.

The overall objective is, of course, to generate confidence. But what sort of things can we put in our sales letters or proposals which will do this? The following is a simple guide to what works and what doesn't when trying to convince prospects that we will keep our promises:

Heart-warmers

- Evidence of financial stability
- An understanding of the customer's needs
- An illustration of our relevant skills and resources
- A description of our support organisation, with the names and phone numbers of key managers
- Reference accounts in the same line of business as the customer
- A local office in the town

(Quite probably in that order of priority.)

Yawns

- Company history since 1852
- A list of inventions and company 'firsts'
- The market research we commissioned which proves we're market leaders
- Mission statements

- Our chief executive's OBE
- Offices in the 78 countries where our customer doesn't operate
- How many of our grommets are used by NASA
- Our sports sponsorships

(Who cares? None of this does anything for the customer.)

This explains why it's very unwise to rely on handing out copies of our glossy Annual Report. It has usually been written for quite a different Audience – our shareholders and investors.

WHAT DO WE MEAN BY AUDIENCE?

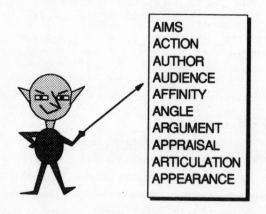

AIMS
ACTION
AUTHOR
AUDIENCE
AFFINITY
ANGLE
ARGUMENT
APPRAISAL
ARTICULATION
APPEARANCE

We define the Audience as 'the person(s) or entity selected as the agency for the Action'. The trick is to decide 'whose cage to rattle to get what we need'. The criteria for selecting an Audience are:

1. **Competence** – Can the Audience deliver what we're asking for?

2. **Motivation** – Can they be motivated to do it for the Author?

If we are sure of both, then we have our Audience. Usually, though, we find that one or the other is missing.

COMPETENCE

Common sense says that we should only ask our audience to do something if they can actually do it:

From: Training Manager
To: Sales Support Manager

As you know, we in Training have made tremendous efforts to put together a sales training course, and unfortunately this has consumed most of our budget. We are therefore asking you if you feel able to make a financial contribution.

From: Sales Support Manager
To: Training Manager

Sorry. I'm already overdrawn at the bank.

This is the Sales Support Manager's mischievous way of telling the Training Manager that she doesn't control the Sales budget. She can't deliver, even if she wanted to. She is the wrong Audience, as only the Sales Director can sanction this expenditure. The Training Manager might try the following approach instead:

From: Training Manager
To: Sales Support Manager

Thanks for your witty response. Could you put my suggestion to your Sales Director?

Now the Sales Support Manager has something she can actually do. However:

From: Sales Support Manager
To: Training Manager

Yes. Of course I could. But I don't intend to.

So the Training Manager decides to target the Sales Director directly:

From: Training Manager
To: Sales Director

As you know, we in Training have made tremendous efforts to put together a sales training course, and unfortunately this has consumed most of our budget. We are therefore asking you whether Sales is able to make a financial contribution.

Before he sends it, however, he spots the Goblin . . .

"Why is he asking *me* to sort him out? Does his director know he's written this?"

He has to change the Author. So he drafts a note for the Personnel Director to send instead.

From: Personnel Director
To: Sales Director

As you know, our Training department have made tremendous efforts to put together a sales training course, and unfortunately this has consumed most of their budget. I have looked carefully at the position, but I am unable to provide any additional funds for training this year. I am therefore asking you whether Sales might feel able to make a financial contribution.

This is much better. The memo now has the authority of the Personnel Director behind it, and it spells out clearly that the Personnel department has exhausted its own resources before approaching Sales.

However, the Training Manager feels there is still something missing. In fact, he can predict the following response:

From: Sales Director
To: Personnel Director

I am sorry your people are in this position. I have similar problems with my own budget. Good luck.

What this lacks, he thinks, is a degree of 'persuasion'.

MOTIVATION

The training Manager starts again, this time trying to create a link between the Action required and the interests of the Audience.

From: Personnel Director
To: Sales Director

As you know, our Training department have made tremendous efforts to put together a sales training course, and unfortunately this has consumed most of their budget. I have looked carefully at the position, but I am unable to provide any additional funds for training. We are therefore faced with having to suspend the courses for the rest of this year. I know you would want the training courses to continue, so I am asking whether you are in a position to help out financially.

His Audience – the Sales Director – not only might have the budget, he reasons, but he would share the goal of enabling sales training to continue. He has, in other words, both competence and motivation.

A few days later, the Personnel Director receives a reply, and passes it down the line to the Training Manager:

From: Sales Director
To: Personnel Director

Please feel free to cancel the courses. We'll muddle through somehow.

Collapse of Training Manager. Not only has he blown his budget, but he now seems to have a course that nobody wants!

USING THE 10A FORM

Under the Author and Audience sections, we enter the identity of each, their tribal allegiances, and their possible aims. Then we can begin to see where aims coincide or conflict. The Training Manager wasn't using a 10A Form, but if he had, it would be looking something like this:

1. **Aims** (operational objective)
    current sales courses to continue.
2. **Action** (desired effect of the communication)
    Sales to make financial contribution.
3. **Author** (sender of the communication)
    personnel director. tribe = training/personnel. aims = enable sales courses to continue.
4. **Audience** (recipients of the communication)
    sales director. tribe = sales. aims = increase sales/ effective sales force/conserve Sales budget.

As we shall see in the next chapter, the Sales Director's polite refusal had something to do with the Aims, and the relationship of the expressed Action to them.

SUMMARY

- Decide whom the Author represents
- Give the Author's credentials
- Note the Author's 'tribes' and aims
- Identify the Audience and whom they represent
- Ensure 'competence'
- Ensure 'motivation'
  - Identify the tribes and aims for the Audience
  - Compare respective aims and check for conflict
- Be prepared to come back and change Author or Audience if subsequently you cannot find an effective Affinity (dealt with in the next chapter)

6. Affinity

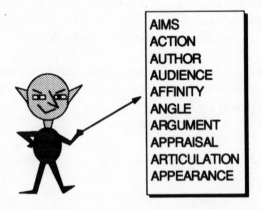

AIMS
ACTION
AUTHOR
AUDIENCE
AFFINITY
ANGLE
ARGUMENT
APPRAISAL
ARTICULATION
APPEARANCE

Towards the end of the last chapter, we came up against the problem of motivating our Audience.

We have a choice: we can order or we can persuade.

Bryan recalls the problems which arose when the wrong choice was being made unintentionally:

I was once manager of a marketing department responsible for a number of new product developments.

Each product manager was responsible for monitoring his own projects. This involved liaison with other divisions within the company and with outside suppliers to ensure that actions were being followed through and timescales met. However, regardless of the effort put in by the product managers in meetings and letters, deadlines were being missed, and programmes were slipping. To put this right, I decided to take on a full-time 'progress-chaser' – Steve – to keep tabs on all the projects.

When Steve arrived, he first spent some time looking back through the correspondence files on each project. He then said he thought he had discovered the problem, but would only tell me what it was when he had corrected it.

Six months later, all projects were firmly on track. After a review one day, I reminded Steve that he had promised to tell me where we had been going wrong. He opened some files and showed me correspondence written by the product managers. They were memos which began 'Please ensure that . . .', or 'We are very concerned to see . . .', or 'Unless you take steps to . . .'.

He pointed out that, to the recipients, they all sounded threatening. 'You chaps have been pointing a gun at their heads,' he commented.

He then showed me a typical memo which he had sent. It began with a brief reminder of the objective of the project, and the progress which had been made so far. It then outlined the problem, explained why it was damaging the project as a whole, and suggested a course of action. The memo ended with the words 'Let us all work together to bring the work back on schedule.'

'This one tells them they're part of our team,' he explained.

ORDERING

Asking or telling someone to do something without explaining why is not the most effective way of achieving business objectives. Implicit in any order is an assumption ('This is what we pay you for . . .') and a promise or threat ('We will reward/punish you if you comply/don't comply'). For it to work, the author has to have the power to follow through on promises or threats. Thus it's normally based upon a formal relationship between author and audience, such as one expressed in a job description, a reporting structure, or a legal contract.

Such a basis for motivation may work sometimes within a tribe, but it's notoriously unreliable outside a tribe. It is normally greeted with indignation or resentment. (Any trainee salesperson who has inadvertently used the words 'You must . . .' with their prospect will know what we mean!) The buyer who treats suppliers as disobedient employees is storing up trouble. They will do as little as possible to stay in line, and will get their own back financially as soon as an opportunity presents itself.

PERSUASION

A persuasive argument will explain how the requested action will contribute to an aim which is acceptable to the audience. It is therefore based on the perceived benefit for the author, the audience, or both. We call this relationship the Affinity.

In each case, the Affinity depends upon respective aims being shared, or at least compatible. If the aims of the author are in conflict with those of the audience, there is no Affinity, and therefore no scope for persuasion. All we can do is order, or threaten. If we want to persuade, the only thing we can do is go back and change Aims, Action, or Author or Audience until we have an Affinity.

There are three important points to bear in mind:

1. In any given situation, there is usually more than one possible Affinity
2. Affinities can be permanent, or they can change according to circumstances – sometimes, they exist only temporarily
3. It's the responsibility of the author to identify, choose and express the Affinity (or Affinities) in the message itself

TYPES OF AFFINITY

There are just three types of affinity

- **Pleading**
- **Selling**
- **Teamwork**

Associated with each one is a form of request which can be used to identify it and distinguish it from the others. The request will not only help us crystallise the affinity on the 10A Form, but it will also become a starting point for the argument later.

Pleading Affinity

With this affinity, we, the author, are expecting the audience to do something for our benefit. The request for this affinity is 'please help to' achieve an objective owned by the author, but compatible with one owned by the audience. We want the audience to come to our aid, but with no expressed benefit for our audience.

Of all the affinities, this is the one that everybody is familiar with. After all, it's the affinity that we learn as a child: 'Help me, Mummy . . .'. It is essentially self-centred – when we want something, it's the one that most of us turn to first. Unfortunately, it's generally the least effective in business. Some individuals may help us out of the goodness of their heart, or because they jump at the chance to demonstrate a special expertise, but it's not wise to rely on it. There is also the problem of low priority – they may have more pressing things on their agenda.

Selling Affinity

The Selling Affinity describes the case when our proposition will be of some benefit to the audience. The associated request is 'let me help you to' achieve an aim which is owned by the audience, but compatible with one owned by the author. The audience is working towards some goal, and the author is providing the means to achieve it. While professional sales staff are trained to use this affinity, it does not come easily to most of us in business. It requires us to stand aside from our self-centred point of view and look at life through the eyes of our audience.

The Selling Affinity is stronger than the Pleading Affinity, since it appeals directly to the self-interest of the audience. There are, however, two major risks; suspicion and alternatives. Since a Selling Affinity need not spell out the author's aims, the audience may become suspicious about the author's motives. In a normal sales situation, both parties know the benefit to the salesman is a sale but, in other cases, the audience will be wondering what's in it for the author.

The risk of alternatives is present because the audience may see other ways of achieving the stated goal, and not necessarily those offered by the author. Just like a salesman, we have competition.

Teamwork Affinity

A Teamwork Affinity is used when both author and audience have identical aims. We can express a Teamwork Affinity in a request which says 'let's both work together to' achieve a shared aim. Both author and audience are strivers towards a common goal. They are pulling in the same direction.

This affinity can be a difficult one to use, since it forces us to lift our focus beyond our own immediate objectives and look for higher aims which both we and our audience can share. The Teamwork Affinity is, however, the strongest of the three. It appeals to a sense of belonging and a desire to cooperate, and the only real risk is a lack of credibility: will the audience accept the author's statements about shared aims? It also has the subtle advantage that if the proposition goes horribly wrong, all parties can demonstrate they did it for the right reasons.

AIM HIGH!

The idea is to go for the strongest possible affinity in any situation, and this requires careful thought about respective aims.

The concept of the tribe can help us think about what the tribal aims might be. But we should not infer from tribal membership alone that aims will necessarily be identical, compatible or even incompatible. This will depend on the particular mountain being climbed. The basic strategy is to find aims which are identical, or at least compatible, regardless of the tribes involved. The reality of business life is a constantly shifting mix of goals and alliances, and this gives us plenty of scope for developing aims which can be shared.

To give a simple example of Affinities at work, we'll take the case of the Financial Controller who has a problem with overdue accounts. He is making a speech at a sales conference with the idea of enlisting the help of the sales force.

PLEADING AFFINITY?

If he used a Pleading Affinity, he would simply ask for assistance: 'It's my job to improve the company cashflow. I need your help.' The risk here is flimsy motivation. The sales staff see no immediate benefit to themselves. Their priority is selling and earning commission, not chasing late payments. (In fact, many sales people dislike following up bad debts, simply because they're used to Selling Affinities with their customers, and debt collection involves threatening or, at best, a Pleading Affinity.)

SELLING AFFINITY?

Next, the Controller might try a Selling Affinity: 'Here's an excuse to go and see all your customers and close some repeat business.' The risks in a Selling Affinity are, as we have seen, suspicion and along with it, alternatives. Obviously the audience needs to be comfortable that the respective aims are indeed compatible. A suspicious voice in the audience could well ask: 'Why are you suddenly being so good to us?'

Besides this, the audience may see other ways of achieving their objectives. The voice from the floor could reasonably point out that they already have ample reasons to call on their customers to discuss repeat business.

TEAMWORK AFFINITY?

Finally, the Teamwork Affinity. The only real risk in promoting a Teamwork Affinity is a lack of credibility. Do we have the authority to speak on behalf of the tribe, and to make statements about shared aims? For example, the Controller could say 'We should all pull together to reduce overdue accounts.' 'And which bit are you pulling?' asks the voice in the audience.

This message from this particular author lacks credibility with this particular audience. To work, it needs to come from the Sales Director, the chief of the Sales tribe, and not the Controller. With this simple change of Author, the Controller would probably achieve his objective.

MULTIPLE AFFINITIES

Although the strongest affinity is the one to go for, there will be comparatively few cases where a Teamwork Affinity can be sustained throughout a communication. These would normally be exhortations to teamwork, and with very simple and brief arguments. What do we do if the Teamwork Affinity runs out of steam? And if we have to drop down to another type of affinity, how can we beef it up?

Example

The Marketing department is becoming edgy about the delay in new brochures for a product which is due for launch. They want Printing Services to hurry up.

It would be difficult to use a Teamwork Affinity exclusively: 'Let's both work together to produce the brochures on time . . .' as it's Printing Services' function to get them printed, not Marketing's. On the other hand, a Pleading Affinity on its own would lack strength: 'Please help us in Marketing to have brochures ready in time . . .' Printing Services may have a rush job to reprint internal telephone directories following last week's reorganisation.

In cases like this, we use more than one affinity. We can, say, introduce the subject with a Teamwork Affinity (to remind the audience of the big picture), then present the proposition using a Pleading Affinity (to ask for help), and end up with a Teamwork Affinity again to leave the audience with a feeling that they ought to cooperate. The bare bones of the argument are:

1. **Teamwork Affinity** – 'The company is about to launch an important new product . . .' (An appeal to the company tribe.)
2. **Pleading Affinity** – 'Please speed up the printing of the new brochures . . .' (A request for help to the Printing Services tribe.)
3. **Teamwork Affinity** – 'We will all benefit from a successful launch of the new product . . .' (An appeal again to the company tribe.)

When developed into a memo, the result could be something along these lines:

From: **Marketing Director**
To: **Printing Services Manager**

The company is about to launch the new product range next month, and the lateness of sales brochures is causing us all some concern.

We would be grateful if you could investigate the position as a matter of priority and take appropriate action to expedite printing and distribution within the next week.

We will all benefit if the new product launch is supported by top quality sales and promotional aids.

This is a classic formula, and it can be used in a large number of cases where we need to motivate another tribe within the overall company tribe.

UPGRADING AFFINITIES

Affinities can change over time. This is especially true of the Selling Affinity. Once the sale is made, the relationship between seller and buyer changes subtly. The buyer is under constant pressure to make the product deliver the benefits he promised his company, and the seller is obliged by his company to make the contract stick. Both seller and buyer then have identical aims. They have to make the proposition work, and this usually leads to a potential Teamwork Affinity: 'Let's work together to keep your people and my people happy . . .'. For this reason, many companies employ two distinct types of sales team, one to sell to new accounts, and another to look after existing customers. One uses Selling Affinities, the other can also use a Teamwork Affinity.

An affinity can often be upgraded during a protracted sale, with the salesman putting himself on the same side as the buyer. This can be very effective when negotiating prices: 'I know you would like a

30 per cent discount, but I can tell you our Financial Controller will never agree to that. I'd say the best we could go for would be 20 per cent. We'll try that, if you like.'

Note the use of 'we', suggesting a Teamwork Affinity ('Let's work together to wrap up this contract. . .'). But it can only be used when the customer wants the product (the alternatives having been discarded), and a working relationship has been established (the salesman has enough credibility for teamwork). This is why the smart salesman tries to postpone such negotiations for as long as possible: 'First, you decide whether you want it. Then we'll discuss terms . . .'.

The same technique can be used by the buyer: 'I know you're asking ten million, but I couldn't possibly put that to our bankers. Let's work out something they would be happy with . . .'. The clever buyer, of course, prefers this discussion up front, when he can remind the seller that he still has alternatives.

Who said business can't be fun?

GOALS OR THREATS?

Until now, we have painted a picture of the parties striving towards a particular goal. However, the affinity can also take a negative form. That is, either the author, the audience, or both, can be attempting to avoid a 'threat'. We strongly suggest, therefore, that the objective is expressed in a positive form wherever possible. Most audiences don't like bad news, and tend to shoot the bringers of same.

A new market initiative should therefore try to express positive benefits (increased revenue, higher profits, greater market share, or whatever) rather than frighten the audience by talking about the catastrophe which will envelop them all if the advice is not taken. Audiences soon learn that the sky doesn't fall in if they take no action.

HANDLING COMPLAINTS

The Affinity concept can be very helpful when we're trying to handle a complaint. Most complainants don't make a distinction between the audience and their problem. In effect, they see the audience as the aggressor, and themselves as victim:

From: Novelist
To: ABC Customer Support

I protest at the behaviour exhibited by your frightful ABC word-processing system. When I had the audacity to attempt to print a very long chapter from my new blockbuster, the screen went blank. Nothing happened, except that I lost a complete day's labour. I would deem it a personal favour if you would take your alleged word-processing software and disappear up your nearest mouse port...

How can the customer support representative reply to the letter? What possible affinity can there be here? To handle the complaint, he must move from being the aggressor, to simply being the unwitting means. It was not his intention to create this problem. From there, he can change role again, and help the audience towards their objective:

From: ABC Customer Support
To: Novelist

I am very sorry you have had this problem. On this occasion it would seem that your copy of ABC is one of a small batch which, we have just discovered, accidentally went out with a known bug in it. I have made arrangements for an updated copy to be sent to you by courier. I am sure this will solve the problem, and allow you to complete your novel with no further difficulty.

There is a corollary to this: when making complaints ourselves, we should make it easy for the other person to help us, rather than make allegations about their parentage. The letter of complaint above would have caused less gritting of teeth if it had been written thus:

From: Novelist
To: ABC Customer Support

There is a problem with your ABC word-processing system. When I tried to print out a very long chapter from the typescript of my new novel, the screen went blank. Nothing happened, except that I lost a day's work. I would be grateful if you could look into this for me as a matter of some urgency . . .

Not half as satisfying, but maybe more productive, if only because it expresses a Pleading Affinity, and suggests how the audience should respond.

USING THE 10A FORM

The Affinity section on the 10A Form allows us to make a brief note of the affinity to be used, together with the corresponding request to suit the situation. For example:

5. **Affinity** (relationship between author and audience)
   pleading: "Please help me get my system working."

This type of request should express an objective which is consistent with (identical or contributing to) the Aims of the communication, and with the aims set out under Author. It should not conflict with any Audience aims.

Or:

5. **Affinity** (relationship between author and audience)
   selling: "Let me help you plan for your retirement."

In this case, the request should express an objective which is consistent with one or more of the Aims listed under Audience.

Or:

5. **Affinity (relationship between author and audience)**
   teamwork: "Let's work together to increase
   productivity."

With a Teamwork Affinity, the request should express an objective which is consistent with the Aims of the communication, and with one or more of the aims under Author and Audience.

Thus besides functioning as a reminder, the 10A Form entries under Affinity are intended as a double check that the objectives expressed in the request are indeed identical or compatible, and that they are consistent with the Aims set out previously.

When expressing multiple affinities, we list them in sequence along with their sample requests. In the case of the late sales brochures earlier, the affinities might be annotated on the 10A Form as:

5. **Affinity** (relationship between author and audience)
   teamwork: "Let's work together to launch new
   product."
   pleading: "Please help me to have brochures on time."
   teamwork: "Let's work together to have successful
   launch."

THE FUDDLE STORY CONTINUED

A short while back, we said that if there really is no affinity, then the only thing to do is go back and change Aims, Action, or Author or Audience. Our Fuddle Training Manager has a case in point. The memo which caused the problem was the one he had ghosted for his boss (the Personnel Director) to send to the Sales Director:

From: Personnel Director
To: Sales Director

*As you know, our Training department have made
tremendous efforts to put together a sales training course,
and unfortunately this has consumed most of their budget.*

I have looked carefully at the position, but I am unable to provide any additional funds for training. We are therefore faced with having to suspend the courses for the rest of this year. I know you would want the training courses to continue, so I am asking whether you are in a position to help out financially.

This brought the response:

From: Sales Director
To: Personnel Director

Please feel free to cancel the courses. We'll muddle through somehow.

After the initial shock has worn off, the Training Manager picks up the phone and calls the Sales Support Manager in a discreet attempt to find out why the Sales Director is taking such a bloody-minded attitude. The Sales Support Manager tells him what we already know from the previous chapter, that there have been a number of complaints about the courses. No, she's not going to be specific. No, she's not letting on who said what. And no, she personally hasn't any idea what the Training Manager should do about it, beyond the vague suggestion that the courses obviously need improvement. Yes, she's willing to accept that the Training Manager thinks the courses are very good. But who cares if the dog food is wonderful when the dogs themselves don't like it?

Let's use a 10A Form on his problem, and start thinking about possible affinities. Taking his last memo as our starting point, we can 'reverse engineer' his 10A Form (in other words, deduce what he thought he was trying to achieve):

1. **Aims** (operational objective)
   current sales courses to continue.
2. **Action** (desired effect of the communication)
   Sales to make financial contribution.

3. **Author** (sender of the communication)
    personnel director. tribe = training/personnel.
    aims = enable sales courses to continue.
4. **Audience** (recipients of the communication)
    sales director. tribe = sales. aims = ???

At this point the 10A Form forces him to address the problem of motivation. What are the aims of the Sales Director and his tribe?

4. **Audience** (recipients of the communication)
    sales director. tribe = sales. aims = increase
    sales/effective sales force/conserve Sales budget.

As we now know, the Aim (enable sales courses to continue) is not shared by the audience. To make matters worse, the Action (Sales Department to make financial contribution) actually conflicts with the Sales Director's own aim of conserving his budget. When he reaches the fifth 'A', Affinity, he finds that there is none.

He could go back and change the expressed Aim to something the Sales Director might agree with. The only clue he has is something like 'improve sales training'. Is it compatible with his own aim of continuing the courses? If it's the only way he can persuade any more salesmen on to his courses, then, reluctantly, yes.

Is there an affinity here somewhere? Can he ask for help to improve the sales courses? The Training and Sales tribes' aims are now compatible. He wants the Sales Director to give him some funds to improve the training. He has, in effect, a Pleading Affinity: 'Please help me to improve the sales training . . .'. However, this is a weak affinity. The Sales Director might have other more pressing uses for any spare budget.

He should therefore aim a little higher. Does he have, for example, something to 'sell'? Is there a Selling Affinity? Can he assist the Sales Director towards a Sales goal? How about 'let me help you develop a better trained sales force' in return for a financial contribution?

This could work, but there are a couple of problems. The Sales Director might not be convinced that throwing money at Training will necessarily give him a better trained sales force. There are also the usual risks with this type of affinity. The Sales Director could well suspect that Training's aim is to relieve him of precious budget, and he always has alternatives. After all, he could head-hunt some superstars from a competitor, or if training were really such a good idea, he could use his budget to buy it from an outside consultancy.

The next option is a Teamwork Affinity. What we are trying to achieve is an affinity where both parties are pulling in the same direction. To reach this level, the aims must be identical, and it helps if the Training Manager can show that the tribes are the same. Can he use the idea of creating an effective sales force as a Fuddle tribe aim? Yes. But can the author now share the aims of this 'effective sales force'? Arguably the author as Personnel Director might, but not the Training Manager. His aims are to enable the sales courses to continue, or if he's pushed, to improve sales training.

In fact, expressing this Aim (an effective sales force) might provoke a discussion with a wider agenda. This could end up with the Personnel Director and the Sales Director both agreeing that the best way of achieving 'effective sales force' would be new hirings or to buy the training in from outside, as we noted earlier. In the end, either of these might well be the best answer, but the Training Manager believes in his courses. He's not about to give up and offer his head to the guillotine.

Is there a way of keeping these alternatives off the agenda? Supposing we amend the aims slightly to the immediate and short-term 'increase effectiveness of existing sales force' and point to the need to do this urgently? The Sales Director couldn't argue with that. It might also exclude not only recruitment, but also an outside provider. Tenders, quotations, negotiations and contracts all take time.

However, there is still a difficulty with the Action. How does the financial contribution that Sales are to make help with the Aim to 'increase effectiveness of existing sales force'? The link is decidedly tenuous, and it still conflicts with the Sales aim of holding on to their own budget. This is unfortunate, to say the least. After all, it was the whole reason for writing the memo in the first place!

Can we change the Action? If Sales won't make a donation, what might they be prepared to do instead? Might they provide resources, for instance? If the Training Manager can get Sales actively involved in revising the sales training courses for their own benefit, they may well end up actually wanting to use them. Then, if it turns out that more budget is needed, they might then provide it, or at least make a joint submission with Personnel to get some from somewhere else.

Now the only remaining query is the issue of credibility. The Training Manager had already decided the author should be the Personnel Director, and this turns out to have been a good decision. Although the Sales Director would probably not accept tribal statements from the Training Manager, he should accept them from one of his peers, a member of the board.

We can also reinforce the affinity if we can point to some earlier successful example of cooperation. (The Training Manager heard that the Personnel Director and the Sales Director conspired together to sneak in some extra salesmen during the recruitment freeze some while ago. Perhaps he could use that.)

So what does his 10A Form look like now?

1. **Aims** (operational objective)
   ~~enable sales training to continue.~~ *increase effectiveness of existing sales force.*
2. **Action** (desired effect of the communication)
   ~~Sales to make financial contribution.~~ *Sales to provide resources to improve current training.*
3. **Author** (sender of the communication)
   personnel director. tribe = training/personnel/ *Fuddle.*
   aims = enable sales courses to continue/*increase effectiveness of existing sales force.*

4. **Audience** (recipients of the communication)
   sales director. tribe = sales/*Fuddle*. aims = increase
   sales/effective sales force/conserve Sales
   budget/*increase effectiveness of existing sales force.*
5. **Affinity** (relationship between author and audience)
   *teamwork: "let's work together to increase
   effectiveness of existing sales force for Fuddle ..."*
   (previous e.g. = recruiting problem)

Incidentally, when making revisions to the 10A Form, we don't delete any previous entries. We strike them through, but leave them legible. Revisions can occasionally become complicated, and it's useful to have a kind of log of where we have already been.

The Training Manager's final 10A Form would turn into a memo along these lines:

From: Personnel Director
To: Sales Director

As board directors, we both understand that it is a top priority for the company that our existing sales force operates at peak productivity in these difficult times. One of the key contributing factors to their effectiveness should be training, and I think we are both very concerned that the current courses are apparently not meeting the needs of the sales force. I therefore propose that our departments work together on this to see how the present training might be improved. I realise that both our budgets are fully stretched, and that we may therefore have a funding problem. When we have agreed on the requirement, I suggest we consider making a joint approach to the MD for additional funds, if necessary. (Remember when we successfully obtained some more heads for you during the recruitment freeze last year?)

From: Sales Director
To: Personnel Director

Great minds think alike! My Sales Support Manager is already looking at the situation, and she will contact someone in your department in the next day or so.

Note

Just two points. Firstly, in the worked example, the planning of the communication actually caused the Training Manager to change his objectives. Are we seriously suggesting that the communication should dictate what we're trying to achieve? Isn't this the 'cart before the horse'? Where does it say any of this in the management training manuals?

The point is this. If we cannot manage our message so that we can motivate others, then we may as well not bother. Business, like politics, is the art of the possible. If the Training Manager couldn't find a way of getting Sales to pay for his own bad budgeting, so what? Instead, the 10A Technique helped him identify what he could – and should – be doing to progress the interests of the parties involved. Anyway, along the way, he probably saved his own bacon.

Secondly, we fully recognise that the Affinity concept is open to abuse. It is easy to assume we can hide our true aims from our audience, and devise identical or compatible aims to get what we want. But if our real aims conflict with the interests of the audience, then we stand little chance of getting away with it more than once.

SUMMARY

- Look at the respective 'tribes' for Author and Audience
- Establish identical or compatible Aims
- Identify the Affinity or 'perceived benefit' relationships
- Go for the highest Affinity possible
  - teamwork, then
  - selling, then
  - pleading
- Try using multiple Affinities when pleading or selling
- Point to some evidence of a previous successful Affinity
- If no Affinity, change Aims, Action, Author or Audience!

In the Appendix, you will find a graphic called the Affinity Model. It summarises the key points about Affinities in pictorial form and can be used for quick reference.

7. Angle

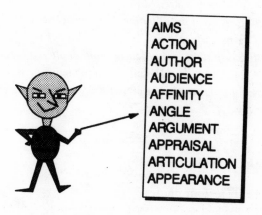

AIMS
ACTION
AUTHOR
AUDIENCE
AFFINITY
ANGLE
ARGUMENT
APPRAISAL
ARTICULATION
APPEARANCE

We've seen (Chapter 6) how Affinities can help us understand and define the motivating relationship between the author and the audience. We have thus laid the foundations for building the persuasive argument. The next question to be addressed is: 'How do we actually use it in practice?' It's all very well having a picture in our minds of the affinity, but how do we go about expressing it?

This is where Angle comes in. By Angle, we mean the standpoint from which we view and express the argument. The process of building a case based upon the affinity can be made very simple by choosing the right angle or point of view. The angle forces us to view things in such a way that the affinity comes through almost of its own accord. On the other hand, all the effort we made to come up with the right affinity will be wasted if we get the angle wrong.

Bryan has a very simple real-life example of how the careless use of personal pronouns can express the wrong Affinity entirely:

> When ICL took over Singer Business Machines in the 1970s, it acquired a manufacturing facility in Utica in New York State. A full five years after the takeover, I went across with a team of managers from the UK to discuss a possible new development with the people in the plant. They were very helpful and informative, and they certainly wanted the work, but for three days they addressed us as 'you guys from ICL . . .'. The use of "you" (instead of the collective "we") suggested strongly they had rejected the Teamwork Affinity in favour of a Selling Affinity. As a result, we felt suspicion, and began to think of alternatives.
>
> On the flight home, our Product Planning representative announced he was strongly in favour of the project being given to one of 'our own' factories in the UK.

TYPES OF ANGLE

We can choose from four angles:

- **Author-angle**
- **Audience-angle**
- **Shared-angle**
- **Neutral-angle**

At this stage of filling in the 10A Form, all we have to do is decide which angle to use, and our choice will depend entirely on the Affinity (or Affinities) we have selected. The conscious adoption of a particular angle will force our mind into a specific point of view. This will help us think of the right Arguments, and when we come to Articulation, it will determine the kind of language we employ.

AUTHOR-ANGLE

Author-angle expresses everything from the author's point of view: 'I'm talking about me.' It can be used when we want to draw the

audience's attention to our own objectives, activities and problems.
It expresses the Pleading Affinity (please help me to . . .). The use of
Author-angle is instinctive for most of us, and does not present us
with any real difficulty. It's what comes naturally, after all.

From: Sales Director
To: IT Manager

I think it would be very useful if I could have regular
reports on sales by customer type in addition to the normal
printouts. This would help me identify where to put our
prospecting effort. Could you please look into the feasibility
of this for me?

The author is making a straightforward request for help, a
Pleading Affinity. The viewpoint adopted is his own, with lots of 'I'
and 'me'. (He could, of course, be speaking for the whole of the Sales
tribe, so that these would be replaced by 'we' and 'us'.) The author
expresses the request in terms of his own needs and wishes.

AUDIENCE-ANGLE

Audience-angle expresses everything from the audience's point of
view: 'I'm talking about you.' Audience-angle is strongly advised
when we are trying to sell a proposition or product, and we need to
create an impression of sympathy and understanding. This makes it
particularly suitable for sales letters, proposals, handling complaints,
counselling and teaching. Audience-angle is used to put across the
Selling Affinity ('let me help you to . . .').

From: Insurance salesman
To: Prospect

Allied Mutual has a range of insurance products
specifically intended for people like yourself, including an
income protection plan which will guarantee your peace of
mind if you become disabled through illness or accident. If

you would like to hear more about how Allied Mutual can help you, please fill in the reply-paid card and return it to us.

This is the voice of the authentic sales representative. His basic training drums into him the crucial importance of explaining what his products can do for the client. Note the frequent use of 'you' and 'yours'.

The same angle, however, can be used by anybody in business situations, salesperson or not. For example, the request for more printouts just now could be answered like this:

From: IT Manager
To: Sales Director

In answer to your request for more sales statistics, you will find that the best solution would be for you to have your own sales analysis system. Once a month, we can let you have the complete sales order file on a diskette which you can load into one of your PCs. Then you can look up whatever you want, and whenever you want. If you are not sure what you need, I have made out a requisition for the hardware and software for you. Just sign it, and we'll take care of the rest. When it's delivered, we'll come over and help you get started.

The IT Manager has used the same Audience-angle to sell the solution to the Sales Director. He expresses everything in terms of the Sales Director and his aims. Where the IT Manager does appear, it's only to help. He may well have other objectives, but he doesn't spell them out. Note that his decision to use Audience-angle forced him to think what else he could say to reinforce it, and he came up with the idea of enclosing a completed requisition. He probably didn't fill it in himself, nor did he have any intention of popping across in person to show the sales people how to use the new system. That was beside the point – he created an impression of helpfulness.

The use of Audience-angle is not intuitive, since we are naturally self-centred. We have to make a conscious effort to ignore our own standpoint and put ourselves in the shoes of the audience. Audience-angle, however, is powerful and can be very persuasive whenever we need to sell our proposition.

SHARED-ANGLE

Shared-angle expresses everything from the viewpoint of both author and audience: 'Let's talk about us.' Shared-angle shows a common purpose, and creates an atmosphere of cooperation. We use it to convey the Teamwork Affinity ('let's both work together to . . .'). It's the one to adopt when addressing our own department, or people working towards a common goal within the organisation.

From: Sales Director
To: All sales staff

The IT department has organised a new sales analysis system for our benefit. It is important that we all operate at peak effectiveness during these difficult times, and this includes making full use of the prospecting information available to us. Our system arrives on Friday, so I would like you all to join me at 4 p.m. for some personal hands-on instruction on how to use it.

He has painted a picture of cooperation and common objectives, characterised by the frequent mentions of 'we', 'us' and 'our'. Both author and audience are inseparable.

As in the preceding example, the use of the right angle led to the right argument. The Sales Director decided (quite correctly) to adopt Shared-angle as being the most effective way to motivate his people, and found himself writing the words 'for our benefit'. The thought then struck him: 'How will the department see it's for my benefit as well as theirs?' So he included himself in the training session. And why not? He might learn something! Again, Shared-angle doesn't come naturally, but is a strong force for motivation if applied correctly.

NEUTRAL-ANGLE

Neutral-angle takes a viewpoint independent of both author and audience, and is a bird's-eye-view of the situation. We use it when the audience is only interested in facts and authoritative interpretation, as in reportage, histories, research, investigation and instructions:

> *The correct procedure in respect of applications for employment is that the candidate attends an introductory seminar. This is to allow him/her to acquire an appreciation of the company and its products before progressing to the formal interview phase.*

This message does not overtly assign roles to the author or audience, or even mention them. This is a good idea when the author is irrelevant and the audience could be anybody. It's also the one to use when the audience is interested in the objective truth. The appearance of personalities would introduce motivation issues, suggesting bias.

Neutral-angle does, therefore, have a part to play in persuasion. Since it describes facts, it can generate credibility by distancing the author and his or her objectives from the matter under discussion.

Let us go back to our insurance salesman. He could have given his letter a little more authority by introducing the subject with a Neutral-angle sentence:

From: Insurance salesman
To: Prospect

Neutral-angle:

Statistics show that the vast majority of self-employed professionals lack adequate permanent health insurance.

Audience-angle:

Allied Mutual has a range of insurance products specifically intended for people like yourself, including an income protection plan which will guarantee your peace of mind.

Beware, however, the temptation to use Neutral-angle when offering opinions or unsubstantiated facts. This is an obvious ploy often used to lend authority to weak reasoning, and it will destroy our credibility.

CHANGE OF ANGLE

As the previous example suggests, very often the angle will change during the argument, and especially when the Affinity changes. The following example starts with Shared-angle (for the Teamwork Affinity), then changes to Author-angle (for a little pleading), and concludes with a final Shared-angle exhortation to reinforce the Teamwork Affinity again:

From: Customer Engineering Manager
To: Manufacturing Quality Assurance Manager

Shared-angle for a Teamwork Affinity:

The company is experiencing problems with the reliability of our product range, and we are losing sales as a result.

Author-angle for a Pleading Affinity:

We would be grateful if you would look urgently at the warranty claims and take the necessary steps to implement any necessary manufacturing changes.

Shared-angle for a Teamwork Affinity:

It is vital that the company continues to enjoy a reputation for top quality products.

A change of angle might also be needed when making a complaint. We could use a Neutral-angle statement to grab attention, then an Author-angle description of events, followed by a Shared-angle request for cooperation:

From: Customer Services Manager
To: IT Manager

Neutral-angle:

Any company's image is affected by the treatment customers receive when they call for assistance.

Author-angle:

This department functions as the first line of contact. Last Thursday, we found we could not get any of our enquiry workstations on-line. I called the Help Desk, and I was told that we should have received software updates. When we finally tracked them down (wrongly delivered to Admin), I found that they were on 3½″ disks instead of the 5¼″ disks which we use, and we had to transfer them ourselves. As a result, we were totally unable to handle any customer queries for the best part of the day, and we had to field a number of angry complaints.

Shared-angle:

I am sure you will agree that this does nothing for the company's reputation. I gather that other departments have had similar experiences, so I think it might be a good idea for us all to meet to see how we can avoid this problem in future.

We said before that Author-angle is essentially self-centred, and does little to motivate the audience. It can, however, be effective when making complaints. If something is giving us a problem, the chances are that the person we are complaining to doesn't know about it, or may not realise the extent of the effect. Most people genuinely don't want to cause problems, and won't need further motivation to make amends. What is more, the complainant is not just speaking for himself, but for the people in his department (his constituents). It's they who are having to handle the angry customers, and he's obliged to make the case on their behalf as well as his own.

In any event, trying to adopt a more objective standpoint can be tricky in situations like this. We might find ourselves attempting to guess at intention, as well as describing the event and its effect. We may not know exactly how something came to happen. We just know that it did. Telling it from our own angle is the only way we can speak with any authority on the subject. Note that the complainant in the example did not attribute blame or intent, so there is nothing in the memo which the IT manager could dispute, or take exception to.

MISUSE OF AUTHOR-ANGLE

On the other hand, the thoughtless use of Author-angle can wreck the affinity. You recall the letter from the IT Manager quoted earlier? What might he have said if he had used Author-angle instead of Audience-angle?

From: IT Manager
To: Sales Director

Thank you for your enquiry concerning additional sales printouts. Unfortunately, I receive requests just like this twenty times a week, and there is no way I can cope with my existing staff. However, we can download the MSO file every month and distribute it in Lotus WKS format.

Sounds familiar? He has expressed the message entirely from his own point of view, and blithely using his own jargon (download, MSO, Lotus). There is no affinity here. Quite the opposite.

"What on earth is MSO? Lotus WKS? Is that the turbo–charged model? How come we have to make do with Sierras?"

The misplaced use of Author–angle is very common when answering a complaint:

Thank you for your letter. It is my responsibility to ensure that such problems are reported in detail to the Customer Services Manager on a daily basis. It is then up to him to decide on the appropriate action in each case. As a matter of policy, we do not commit ourselves to dates, but we would normally try to answer complaints within five working days.

"So what are you actually going to do about it?"

This sort of atrocity is all too frequent. It comes as a shock to most of us that complaining customers are not in the least interested in our company policy, or whether our computer has broken down, or that we're filling in for the person who usually does the job. Even worse, the letter manages to reveal that the writer is not authorised to take any action, and that the company receives so many complaints that they never feel confident about predicting how long it will take to sort them out.

As we discussed in the chapter on Affinity, it is a good idea when handling complaints to express a Selling Affinity ('let me save you from . . .'). The correct angle should then be Audience-angle:

Thank you for your letter. We are sorry you are having this problem. On your behalf, I will bring it to the attention of our customer services manager immediately and he will look into it for you. You can expect to hear from us within five days.

Nothing has been compromised. The writer has not exceeded his or her authority, nor made any commitment to the customer. Nothing has changed, except that the reader now has the feeling that the writer is working on their behalf, and that something may happen within five days.

Author-angle instead of Neutral

When asked for an objective report, many of us fall into the trap of assuming that the audience is interested in us, rather than the subject:

From: Maintenance Manager
To: Admin Director

In answer to your memo about the lift breaking down again, I'd like to point out that I have been warning about this for some time. I was first called out two months ago when it jammed, and I had to free the occupants. I removed the cover on the control unit and I could see that the circuit-breaker had tripped. I reset it, and the lift then functioned normally. I filled in a report and sent it to the manufacturer. Then, a fortnight ago, there was another message from Sales waiting for me when I arrived at the office. . . .

He is reporting the "facts" as he saw them, but it reads like his personal diary. The Admin Director may find this fascinating, or he may wonder what the Maintenance Manager is covering up. Either way, he's going to find it hard to learn what was actually wrong with the lift.

THE FUDDLE STORY CONTINUES

You will remember that the Sales Director is unhappy about the quality of the existing courses being run by Training, and that the Training Manager – posing as the Personnel Director – has suggested that Sales and Training work together to improve the courses. The Sales Director has agreed.

The Sales Director now wants to hold a meeting of his sales force and the Training Manager to thrash it out. He needs to write a brief memo to his people calling them to the meeting. We can guess that the affinity to use is probably a Teamwork Affinity. But let's take this memo, and see how different Angles can have different effects on the same message.

Author-angle version

For his first attempt, he might not trouble to use persuasion at all:

From: Sales Director
To: All sales staff

I am considering how to improve the sales training course. I want your ideas on this, so I would like you all to meet with the Training Manager and myself to discuss it. I am not prepared to have the normal working week disrupted, so the meeting will be on Saturday morning. Please confirm to Sam that you can attend.

He has created the impression that the sales force exists for his personal benefit, and he has made no suggestion that the exercise is in the salesmen's interests. If he can command this sort of obedience, he might get away with it. The chances are, however, that he would not secure their enthusiastic cooperation. If this is the case, he might then change his mind and try a little persuasion by 'pleading':

I am worried about the effectiveness of the current sales training, and I am holding a meeting with the Training Manager to discuss how to improve it. I really need your support on this, so I would be grateful if you could all attend as well. Because of other commitments, I'm afraid the meeting will have to be on Saturday morning. I would appreciate it if you could confirm to Sam that you can attend.

Sales staff being the soft-hearted folk that they are, he could look forward to a full attendance. Maybe.

Audience-angle version

Next, he might bring to bear his own personal selling skills:

I know you all want to increase your earnings through better sales training. Here is your chance to tell us what you want. Would you all like to join the Training Manager and myself for a meeting to discuss what you think ought to be done about it? I know you will not want to miss any selling time, so I have arranged the meeting for Saturday morning. Would you please confirm to Sam that you can attend.

This time, he has done a selling job on his own tribal braves. However, while there is nothing wrong with the argument, it is likely to provoke some ironic jeers from his hard-bitten salesmen. If the memo had been written (with the appropriate changes) by the Training Manager instead, the impression then created would have been one of sympathy and helpfulness. For the Sales Director to write it to his own people is a waste of a perfectly good Teamwork Affinity.

Shared-angle

We all want to increase our earnings through better sales training. The whole department has ideas on what we need, so would you join the Training Manager and myself for a meeting to discuss what we can do about it? We are all very busy at the moment, so it will have to be on Saturday morning. Please confirm to Sam that you can attend.

He has used Shared-angle to reflect the Teamwork Affinity. As we noted earlier, this is the strongest form of affinity to use, and in this example, would motivate the audience. Since the author is the Sales Director, he is running little risk of lacking credibility. After all, he's the chief of the tribe.

Neutral

As an afterthought, he decides to send a note to the Personnel Director, for information only. For this, he produces a Neutral-angle version:

As you know, there is a need to improve the sales training course, and some sales staff have indicated that they have suggestions to make. There will be a meeting on Saturday between all sales staff and the Training Manager to discuss it.

This is written from an objective viewpoint. It is a flat statement of the facts, with no attempt to motivate: it's ideal for a situation report. But if it had been sent to his sales staff, it would have run the same risks as the Author-angle version. There could well be an epidemic of toothache, terminally-ill grandmothers, or flat batteries when Saturday morning arrived.

Meanwhile, he has also sent an invitation to the Training Manager. The Training Manager, however, has other plans for his weekend. He reaches promptly for his keyboard and types:

From: Training Manager
To: Sales Director

In response to your memo about a meeting to discuss sales training with you and your sales force, I am afraid that Saturday morning is totally out of the question. Saturday is the day my golf club is holding its annual tournament, and as club secretary, I am responsible for organising the event. Tuesday would suit me admirably.

He then pauses. This is pure Author-angle, but without a Pleading Affinity. How can he rewrite the memo using a different angle so he can still go to the golf club without running the risk of personal injury from the Sales Director? Can he use Audience-angle to help him sell his absence as a positive advantage to the Sales tribe?

From: Training Manager
To: Sales Director

Thank you for your invitation to discuss sales training with you and your sales force. Normally, I would be delighted to come and hear your views. However, in this case, I know you are keen to have a very frank and productive discussion, and I think you would agree that my presence could have an inhibiting effect on your people. I very much look forward to hearing your conclusions next week.

Audience-angle forced him to see things from their point of view. He realised that they would see the golf tournament as an annoying irrelevance, and managed to come up with what he thought might be a benefit to them instead.

The only problem is the normal one with a Selling Affinity. The Sales Director might suspect that he has something else – not necessarily a golf tournament – lined up for the weekend. The only solution is honesty, but with a Pleading Affinity:

In response to your memo about a meeting to discuss sales training with you and your sales force, I am afraid that Saturday morning would create a problem for me. This is the day my golf club is holding its annual tournament, and as club secretary, I am responsible for organising the event. Would it be possible to rearrange the meeting?

From: Sales Director
To: Training Manager

No.

We never said you could win them all, did we? (At least the Sales Director might respect his honesty.)

SUMMARY

- For a Teamwork affinity ('let's both work together to . . .'), use Shared-angle
  - put both parties in the same boat
  - express the argument in terms of the effect on both parties together
  - use 'we' and 'our'
- For a Selling Affinity ('let me help you to . . .'), use Audience-angle
  - take the action to the audience
  - express it in terms of the effect on the audience
  - leave out anything irrelevant to the audience
  - use 'you' and 'your'
- For a Pleading Affinity ('please help me to . . .'), use Author-angle
  - explain why you need help or saving
- For extra credibility in an argument:
  - use Neutral to discuss facts or evidence
  - move to another angle for the proposition
- Apply the angle to a key sentence – This forces your mind into the right viewing position, and gets the right arguments flowing

8. Argument – the Compelling Proposition

On the 10A Form, there is a blank space headed Argument. This is where we will be sketching out our message. There are two steps involved. The first is covered in this chapter, where we shall be discovering ways of enriching our proposition. The second is the actual structuring of the argument, and that will be discussed in Chapter 9.

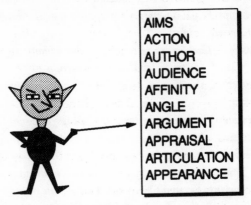

AIMS
ACTION
AUTHOR
AUDIENCE
AFFINITY
ANGLE
ARGUMENT
APPRAISAL
ARTICULATION
APPEARANCE

The exact nature of what we are proposing will depend on individual circumstances. No planning technique can replace the author's experience and judgement when it comes to developing solutions to real problems, and the 10A Technique is not intended to.

What it will do is help us make the best use of our arguments, to express them clearly and convincingly. It will also stimulate us to think about a few matters that otherwise might not occur to us, such as the hidden objections the audience may prefer not to reveal.

Jim recalls just such a case:

My company had a research department which consisted of one very ambitious young lady. Her job was to watch the press and magazines for relevant news and articles, and to track our competitors' doings. This she did extremely efficiently and single-handedly, apart from the occasional use of a typist from the department next door. To cope with the ever-increasing amount of material, she developed a very sophisticated card-indexing system, but her office was soon bursting at the seams with stacks of press cuttings, brochures, directories, catalogues, and so on. To make matters worse, she was increasingly sending typewritten reports back for correction to the typist who, naturally enough, found it hard to produce columns of figures and complicated technical text without the odd error.

Eventually, someone suggested the IT department might be able to help, and an analyst came over to look at her system in some detail. He prepared a comprehensive report. It proposed that she have a personal computer of her own, with software very similar to her manual card-indexing system. The report described all the advantages of electronic filing, fast quality printouts, and even connection to the on-line news agencies. She could also prepare briefs herself, without having to ask the unfortunate typist.

To everybody's surprise, she turned the proposal down flat. She said that, on reflection, she thought she could manage well enough with her current system.

At this point, I left the company. However, about a year later, I happened to run into her at a conference. During one of the coffee breaks, I reminded her about the offer she had turned down, and asked her why. With some embarrassment, she told me the reason: she had never learned to operate a keyboard. This was a deliberate decision on her part. On leaving college, she had promised herself that she would never learn to type so nobody would ever try to make her become a typist.

This was her only reservation, and the report had failed to anticipate it.

UNIQUE SELLING PROPOSITIONS

Books on selling used to encourage us to find something unique about our proposition. If we could identify something about our product which the competition didn't have, the prospect had no choice other than to buy ours. In this way, we could avoid the risk of alternatives which comes with the Selling Affinity.

It sounds easy in theory, but in practice such uniqueness is elusive, and the tactic relies on the audience sharing our enthusiasm for the differentiator. The engine in our car might uniquely have seven cylinders, but this will mean nothing to the fleet buyer who is mainly interested in low running costs and high residual value.

In business, the most successful propositions are those which, in the mind of the audience, offer the most benefit for the least disadvantage. In this sense, they are therefore not so much unique as the most compelling.

Our starting point, then, is that we have identified both problem and solution. What can we do to make our recommendations as compelling as possible?

PROBLEMS WITH PROPOSALS

Many reports, memos and presentations fall down in two important areas:

1. **They don't make the most of a good proposition** – The author fails to express some key benefits, and relies on the audience to use their own imagination

2. **They fail to address possible reasons for rejection** – In most cases, the author could easily have anticipated objections if only he had thought about them

To avoid these disasters, the 10A Technique offers us these acronyms:

- **SCORE** – which shows how to make our proposition especially attractive
- **STALL** and **FAILURE** – which force us to think about possible reasons for rejection, some of which may never be expressed by the audience!

In order to make a proposition compelling, we need to think about both 'attack' and 'defence'. It's no use charging off like the Light Brigade at a particular objective while ignoring the guns on the hills on either side of us. Thus, SCORE helps us attack, whilst STALL and FAILURE will take care of defence.

How to SCORE

SCORE stands for propositions which are: Synergistic; Compatible; Opportune; Rewarding; Easy.

Synergistic

A synergistic proposition is one which will contribute to the audience's objectives in more than one way. Our case will be even more attractive if we can show how it will contribute to the audience's other objectives. In effect, we are killing several birds with one stone. Examples might include:

- Any way of meeting other known audience objectives (including personal aims like promoting an image of innovation, initiative, forward-thinking etc)
- Using resources (people, skills, equipment, real estate) which are currently redundant
- Acquisition of resources which can be used for other purposes
- Incidentally fulfilling some obligation, such as placing an order with a supplier just rejected for another contract

Compatible

A compatible proposition will be seen to be in line with the audience's normal way of doing things, and will not require the audience to do anything unusual. In effect, killing a bird with the usual stone. Examples are:

- A new venture which is consistent with the company's overall strategy
- A new product which can be sold by the existing sales force
- An unfamiliar task to which existing skills are transferable
- A new procedure which can be accommodated within an existing system

This is also where we might think about applying peer pressure. 'This is exactly the kind of thing companies like ours are now doing . . .'. This where we use reference accounts, if we have any.

Opportune

The commonest escape route from a decision is to postpone it. No matter how hard we work to make our proposal superior, there always remains one alternative for the audience: to do nothing.

The case for an opportune proposition will show how the time is right, and that the time is now. It should never be expressed as an imperative, but by demonstrating the adverse consequences of deferment. For example: 'Act now, we have no choice!' sounds very much like panic. 'We could postpone this for a year, but we believe the competition is already working on something similar' sounds more objective and considered.

Better still, just as we favoured positive expression of Affinities earlier (to avoid being shot for delivering nasty surprises), we should emphasise how conditions are currently more favourable than they have been, or will be in future: 'By acting now, we could achieve a two-year lead over the competition . . .'.

Rewarding

The proposition will spring into life if we spell out the benefits in detail, but how can we do this? The answer is to imagine that the proposition has already been accepted, and then paint a picture of the consequent benefits. Instead of saying:

> The relocation will result in a much more attractive working environment.

. . . add a bit of detail about what it will mean for those affected:

> The offices will be new, pleasantly furnished, and fully-equipped with modern lifts, air-conditioning, and lighting. The lawns will provide an attractive view for those working inside, as well as a staff recreation area during breaks. There will be ample parking for both staff and visitors. For those commuting by public transport, there is a bus stop immediately outside, and the mainline station is ten minutes' walk away. And for shoppers, there is a new precinct within a mile, with most of the major chains and convenience stores.

It sounds like an estate agent speaking, and perhaps it should. Aren't we 'selling' it too?

Easy

We can show how easy the proposition will be to implement. If it really is going to be that simple, then let's say so and, most importantly, sketch out the steps along the way.

One of the justified criticisms of marketing managers (as opposed to sales managers) is that they spend hours making a very sound case for attacking a new market, but give no clue as to exactly how this might be done. They imagine that it's enough to point the way. They see themselves as strategists, rather than tacticians. Fair enough, but they shouldn't be amazed when the sales force decides it looks too difficult and carries on with what they feel comfortable doing. The most professional marketeers are those who accept some responsibility for the 'how' as well as the 'why'. They sketch out a few suggestions about where the market can be found, what makes it tick, and how it might be approached. The sales force then sees that (a) someone understands it, and (b) that it might not be that difficult after all.

At the same time, we should never underplay what the task involves. Most things usually involve effort or are difficult in some way. We are not helping our case if we gloss over problems, since they will either be immediately apparent to the audience, or they will surface later. Either way, the effect will be damaging.

But first, we should distinguish between 'effort' and 'difficulty'. (The difference? Digging the garden requires effort. Getting dressed in the dark is difficult.) We can justify effort, but the audience will resist difficulty.

Everybody will accept that effort will be required. 'No pain, no gain' seems a fair deal. Medals can be awarded. Effort can be sold as the 'investment' needed to achieve the return. If the proposition requires extensive resources over time, then let's make it clear what is involved. If we don't, we won't get them, and then we can't do the job.

Difficulty, however, needs a different approach. If the audience says 'We can see some difficulties in that', they are really saying 'There are some obstacles we may not be able to overcome, regardless of effort'. Our new project may require skills which the company just doesn't have. Or the new product may need to be machined to finer tolerances than our current equipment can cope with, and the machine to do it may not be available anywhere at any price.

In such cases, we should anticipate difficulties, and offer solutions. This shows that we have thought about it, and that we will be around to help when the going gets hard. If the proposition really is too difficult, then it's we who have the problem, and not the audience. We must then go back to the drawing board and tackle the problem a different way. We'll soon acquire a Walter Mitty reputation if we insist on being persuasive about impossible solutions.

A simple SCORE

Imagine a salesman trying to persuade us to buy our partner a new car imported from Ruritania. It is cheap, economical, well-made, and it performs well. We are interested. Then he reinforces his pitch using SCORE:

- **Synergistic** – 'It would make a marvellous birthday present, and you would be supporting the new Ruritanian market economy.'
- **Compatible** – 'It's very similar to your partner's Metro. And I've sold nine already this week, including two to your neighbours down the road.'
- **Opportune** – 'The price goes up on Monday, and the Metro is already ten years old.'
- **Rewarding** – 'Think what a wonderful surprise it would be for your partner. And won't your friends be impressed!'
- **Easy** – 'No deposit, 0 per cent finance, and it's in stock now. All you need to do is sign just here.'

Tempted? Yes, but we can think of a few objections.

A STALLed argument

STALL stands for: Suspicion; Theology; Aberration; Linkage; and Low priority. These represent objections which may or may not be disclosed by the audience.

Suspicion

The audience has some reason to suspect our motives or our judgement, usually because of some previous bad experience. ('The last time we listened to you, we lost five million. How much will it cost us this time?') As we saw earlier, the Selling Affinity runs this risk if the author's aims are not clear to the audience.

Theology

The audience is bound by some edict, standing instruction or prejudice which conflicts with the proposition. For example, the company may have a list of approved suppliers, and the one we want to use isn't on it. Or the proposition challenges some firmly held view: 'We looked at that last year, and decided against it.' Or it may simply be a question of not following an existing authorised procedure.

Aberration

Aberration applies when our proposition is so contrary to normal practice that the audience foresees continually having to justify their decision to others. If it goes wrong, they will appear especially ridiculous. As an example, Sir Clive Sinclair is now best known for his disastrous C5 electric car–cum–tricycle. This was such a spectacular aberration that all the brilliant work he did with hi-fi, pocket calculators and personal computers has been largely forgotten by the general public.

Linkage

The audience is unlikely to commit to a proposition which is dependent on other events, actions or conditions which are yet to occur. Examples of linkage in action are when the product development programme is turned down because the market has not been researched; or approval is withheld for a new IT system because the company reorganisation has not yet been agreed.

Low priority

The audience has other, more important, things to worry about at the moment. (The usual alligators and swamps syndrome . . .) This is a problem with the Pleading Affinity in particular.

The new car has STALLED

The car salesman is reaching for his order pad, but our Goblin has been whispering a few things in our ear. As a result, we find ourselves with the following objections.

- **Suspicion** – 'Aren't you the chap that talked my daughter into buying that Reliant Robin?'
- **Theology** – 'We always buy British.'
- **Aberration** – 'We could never buy one from Ruritania!'
- **Linkage** – 'We would have to sell the Metro first.'
- **Low priority** – 'Anyway, a new Rover for me is top of the list.'

Fairly disheartening for the salesman, but, as we shall see in a moment, there is worse to come.

Doomed to FAILURE

FAILURE represents another set of reasons for rejection. Unlike STALL problems, however, it is quite likely that the audience will never tell us about them. FAILURE stands for: Funding; Abasement; Investment; Lock-in; Uncertainty; Risk; and Expertise.

Funding

Funding is a likely problem during a recession. In good times, funds are normally available if the expenditure can be justified but in bad times funding becomes a sensitive issue. The inability to secure funding suggests a lack of influence. It may also hint at imminent insolvency. For these reasons, we cannot expect the audience to share their lack of confidence with us.

Abasement

Abasement is when the proposition will detract in some way from the audience and their operation. This is especially serious if it involves status and internal 'empires' (headcount, budget, equipment, real estate). This will probably not be disclosed by the audience, because they know they will come across as self-centred, greedy, and more concerned with personal ambition than with the common good.

Investment

Investment relates to a perceived conflict between the proposition and some previous investment or effort. The effect can be serious if the investment is extensive. That is, the audience will have to write off considerable expenditure, disturb well-established procedures, or discard a set of relationships which have been built up over time.

Previous investment is a very powerful force for inertia. Sometimes the audience will not reveal this problem, because they can't see how it can be brought into the scope of the transaction. It's as though the audience had resigned themselves to saying: 'I know it's not your problem, it's mine, so I won't bother to bring it up.'

Lock-in

Lock-in restricts the audience's future choices, and requires a degree of commitment that the audience is not prepared to give. It will be all or nothing. Fear of lock-in is most obvious when a change of supplier is on the table for discussion. The audience is not confident that the new supplier will always be able to come up with the goods, or they suspect that the supplier will take advantage of a captive customer.

As with investment, the fear of lock-in may not be disclosed because the audience can't usually see how it can be made part of the transaction. In the case of a new supplier, for example, expressing a doubt about future capability will only provoke a repeat of the company credentials. Suppose the audience objects: 'But this would

mean I would always have to buy from you in future.' What else can
the audience expect the supplier to say except: 'And what's wrong
with that?'

Uncertainty

In this context, uncertainty covers all areas of doubt which are
external to the argument being made. Typically, this will include any
impending or possible changes to the audience's perception of the
situation, such as a reorganisation, takeover, merger, or even
closure. The audience may, alternatively, be facing promotion,
demotion, or the prospect of being assigned a new function. There is
a chance that budgets may be cut back, or recruitment stopped.

All these possibilities will have consequences affecting aims,
responsibilities, and capabilities. The audience may stay silent over
such things because, again, removing the uncertainty can't be part of
the transaction, and in any event, the move could well be highly
confidential. Uncertainty is present when we hear reactions such as:
'I'm not sure we should be doing this now . . .'.

Risk

Risk is the perception of the consequences if things go wrong. Most
of us are willing to take calculated risks. However, the perceived risk
is less acceptable when matters are beyond the risk-taker's control.
For instance, our key supplier may be taken over by our competitor,
or a software house may fail to keep to its deadlines. These things are
impossible to put right after the event.

Most audiences tend to approach risk by asking: 'What happens
if this goes as wrong as it possibly can?' But note that the question is
normally addressed to themselves, and not us. Once again, the
audience may not share their perception of the risk if they can't see
how we can remove it. Assurances that we will not go bankrupt will
cut no ice. If it were likely, we wouldn't admit it, and if it happened,
we couldn't do anything about it anyway.

Expertise

Expertise covers the audience's inability to discharge their commitments because of a lack of particular skills or expertise, or their perceived inability to acquire them. It can be brought about by any change in the degree or mix of skills required, such as a sudden increase in executive responsibility, or the need to work with a new system or procedure. It can be very powerful at a personal level, when an individual is now required to become adept at unfamiliar activities, such as selling, public speaking, writing, numerical reasoning, keyboarding, foreign languages, and so on. Like Jim's research manager earlier, the audience will probably keep this quiet if they think such an admission would be demeaning.

DEATH OF THE CAR SALESMAN

Our friend is being very persistent with the Ruritanian car. (By the way, we have now discovered that the gearshift is on the wrong side!) We think to ourselves:

- **Funding** – 'We can't afford it.'
- **Abasement** – 'Could we really park it at the golf club alongside the Mercs and Alfas?'
- **Investment** – 'What about all the money we just laid out on a new gearbox for the Metro?'
- **Lock-in** – 'The only way we'll be able to get rid of it is to trade it in for another one.'
- **Uncertainty** – 'We might be made redundant next week.'
- **Risk** – 'Will we be able to get parts if the importer goes bankrupt?'
- **Expertise** – 'Will we be able to operate the gearshift properly?'

We think the salesman won't be able to help with any of these problems, or we suspect he won't give us honest answers. So, unless problems, or we suspect he won't give us honest answers. So, unless we want a complete re-run of the entire sales pitch, we just thank him and walk away.

The car is a very simple illustration of how SCORE, STALL and FAILURE work, but how could they be applied in a business situation? We can demonstrate this by using the Fuddle training saga, so let's bring ourselves up to date with events, to the point where we are ready to look at an Argument.

THE FUDDLE CORPORATION – THE STORY SO FAR . . .

The Sales Director was concerned about the adverse comments he received about the sales training courses being run by Training, and he asked his Sales Support Manager to report on their effectiveness. The Sales Support Manager broke down the task into a number of steps. First, she contacted the Personnel Director to see whether there might be any yardstick by which sales training could be judged. The only suggestion was one she had already thought of – to compare 'before' and 'after' sales performances. Accordingly, she requested some figures from Accounts.

The next step was to obtain the views and suggestions of sales personnel who had been on the courses and those of their managers.

As it happened, Personnel and Training suggested a joint effort to see how the courses could be improved, so the Sales Director organised a meeting on Saturday to discuss the matter. (The Training Manager was invited, but declined to attend.)

At the meeting, the sales personnel who had been on the course voiced a number of criticisms, and there seemed to be complete agreement that it needed changing. In particular, they felt that:

- It was too American and "pushy"
- It was not suitable for the Fuddle products
- It was weak on handling objections
- The material seemed to vary from course to course

- Most sales people found it inconvenient to spend several days off the job
- It was difficult to get to the training centre in the mornings because of the traffic

One of the newer recruits mentioned that her previous company used computer-based training (CBT). She listed some of the advantages:

- The courseware could be tailored to specific businesses and types of product
- Everybody had access to the same material
- The course was student-paced, and everyone could work at their own speed
- Revision was easy
- Students could explore 'what-if' situations
- CBT could be used in the office at any time
- CBT could be done on the office PCs.

Although she couldn't provide all the technical details, her description aroused a great deal of interest. But there was one big snag. While on the course, she'd had a chat with the Training Manager, and asked why Fuddle didn't use CBT. The Training Manager had been very dismissive. He said he had looked at it a couple of years ago, and he'd found it 'childish'. He was sure that sales staff would prefer 'chalk and talk' with open classroom discussion, rather than have a computer say silly things to them like: 'Well done, John. Now wasn't that easy?'

The Sales Director ponders this. He had been hoping he could just pop across and have a chat with the Personnel Director about beefing up the courses. This is now clearly out of the question. Not only is the criticism of the courses very damning, but the preferred solution is likely to get the audience's back up:

"Oh Lord! Not that silly CBT chestnut again!"

As a result, the meeting broke up with the Sales Director asking his Sales Support Manager to prepare a report for him. His intention is to persuade Personnel, and Training in particular, to change their mind and have another look at computer-based training as an alternative to revising the existing courses. The Sales Support Manager knows she could have a fight on her hands. Let's see how she might use SCORE, STALL and FAILURE to make the proposition compelling.

SCORE IDEAS

- **Synergistic** – CBT could be used for other types of training as well as sales training.
- **Compatible** – CBT can be used on existing PCs after they have been upgraded. Also peer pressure as other companies are already doing it.
- **Opportune** – Fuddle needs effective sales training now because of the recession.
- **Rewarding** – Effective training means higher sales. Salesmen will find CBT very convenient, and the Training department can take credit for introducing modern CBT techniques. There will be improved relations between Sales and Training.
- **Easy** – All we're asking for is another look at CBT. We could start by contacting other companies that already use it. Effort? Sales will help. Difficulty? Might need cooperation from IT on technical issues, but we'll obtain that.

That has certainly enriched the case with some additional thoughts which we can use. Now we turn to defence, starting with STALL.

STALL PROBLEMS

What STALL objections can we imagine coming from Training, and how can we counter them? The reason for using STALL is not to find excuses for retreating with our tail between our legs. It's a pre-event planning tool, which helps us to foresee such objections, and then to think of counter-arguments before they are expressed.

- **Suspicion** – Training might see a conspiracy between IT and Sales. Is this some kind of take-over?
  (**Counter** – Training can take the credit. Also Sales will provide some skills resource, and do the ground work involved. We could perhaps use a 'task force' type structure, with Training, IT and Sales all working together.)
- **Theology** – Training have already looked at CBT in the past and rejected it. Task forces are not part of the Fuddle way, and there's no procedure for them.
  (**Counter** – CBT has probably improved since then, and the task force is now a very common approach. It also breaks down communication barriers.)
- **Aberration** – The IT department is involved. Where we came from, training was done by trainers.
  (**Counter** – Computer-based training is now a proven concept.)
- **Linkage** – Supposing IT aren't willing to help?
  (**Counter** – Sales will get help from IT if Training agrees.)
- **Low priority** – Training's priority is solving their budgeting problems.
  (**Counter** – The top company priority is to have a good sales force in the recession.)

Thus STALL can help us 'get our retaliation in first'. But we must be careful not to hand the audience a loaded gun. We should subtly weave the 'counters' into the argument as we go along, but never introduce the subject with: 'I expect you're thinking that this is a crazy thing to do.' The audience might gratefully pull the trigger: 'Actually, I wasn't, but now you've pointed it out . . .'. Pre-empting objections needs very careful handling, and this is particularly true when we address FAILURE problems.

FUDDLE **FAILURE** ANALYSIS

- **Funding** – Yes! They've blown their budget.
  (**Counter** – Training, Sales and possibly IT will contribute people, not cash. If we need funds later, we can make a joint application.)
- **Abasement** – They will have to do a U-turn on CBT. The Training department might fear they will lose their instructors, their classrooms, and even their new building in the town centre. They may well lose control of training altogether.
  (**Counter** – Training may have been right two years ago, but things have changed. Perhaps we can have their instructor on our task force team, and base the project in their building. In any event, Training will still be responsible for training, CBT-based or otherwise.)
- **Investment** – They put a lot of effort into the existing courseware.
  (**Counter** – If we go ahead with CBT, we'll promise to keep the best bits and build on them.)
- **Lock-in** – It may create a precedent for other courses.
  (**Counter** – Not necessarily. We'll only be looking at a sales course initially. We could find that CBT isn't very good for things like business writing. In any event, if we decide CBT is a good idea, we will pilot a trial CBT sales course, and then we can all evaluate it afterwards.)
- **Uncertainty** – Frankly, we don't know about this. There might be another reorganisation in the near future, the recession is causing uncertainty all round.
  (**Counter** – A more effective training program might save Training from the chop.)
- **Risk** – It could all fail disastrously, especially with Sales and IT involved. What do they know about training? How many Training people are needed on the task force? What will the impact be on the normal training schedule?

(**Counter** – If we decide CBT is a good idea, we'll pilot it to make sure it works, and we will provide some very experienced salesmen to help, including Chris, who has used CBT. As regards Training's commitment to the investigation, we'll only need one person. How about the current sales instructor? He has spare time now that he's not running any more sales courses.)

- **Expertise** – The Training department may not have the selling skills to help with an interactive CBT course. They probably don't have much in the way of computer skills either.

  (**Counter** – Sales will provide the sales skills, and we'll arrange for the Training Manager and the instructor to have their own computer appreciation course.)

Piloting is an extremely useful device for overcoming Aberration, Lock-in, Risk and Expertise. Note how successfully the idea of an 'experiment' was used to keep the doubters quiet and slip the TV cameras into the House of Commons. When was the experiment supposed to end? Does anyone remember? Does anyone care?

CROSS CHECKS

By now it should be clear that SCORE, STALL and FAILURE often prompt us to think about the same things under different headings. For example, some of the Compatible ideas (from SCORE) might well have come up under Aberration (from STALL). In fact, all the SCORE factors are covered again in a negative form under STALL or FAILURE. And Uncertainty and Risk (from FAILURE) may bring to mind the same problems.

This is all deliberate. It's intended to provide a degree of cross-checking. If we miss it under one heading, we'll catch it somewhere else. And since SCORE helps with the expression of positive ideas, we can usually find a home there for the counters that we had to find for the essentially negative ideas under STALL and FAILURE.

It is important to remember, however, that the exercise always results in a number of new ideas, some of which may affect the nature of the proposition itself. Such additions and changes should also be put through SCORE, STALL and FAILURE, otherwise the counter to the objection might in itself raise new ones. To assist with this double-check, we recommend using a special form for the whole process, the SSF Form. It lists what the acronyms stand for, and allows sufficient space alongside each item for notes to be made. When the first pass is complete, it's a good idea to run back through the headings again to check that anything new has also been checked. (A specimen SSF Form is included in the Appendix. You might like to have a similar form made up for your own use, or set up as a document in your PC.)

SUMMARY OF NEW IDEAS

Now we have trawled the Fuddle situation using SCORE, STALL and FAILURE, we can examine our catch. What new things did this exercise make us think of?

1. CBT could be used for other types of training as well as sales training.
2. We should use peer pressure in the argument (other companies are doing it).
3. The Training department can take credit for introducing modern CBT techniques.
4. There will be improved relations between Sales and Training.
5. We need to emphasise that the commitment is only to another investigation.
6. We should start by contacting the other companies which use it.
7. Sales will help with the investigation, and maybe do the ground work.
8. We might need cooperation from IT on technical issues, but we'll obtain that.
9. We could use a task force, with Training, IT and Sales all working together.
10. CBT has probably changed since Training rejected it.
11. Using a task force is now a very common approach.

12. It also breaks down communication barriers.
13. We need to point out that computer-based training is now a proven concept.
14. The investigation will need people, not cash.
15. If cash is needed later, we can make a joint application to the MD.
16. The Training Manager may have been right to reject CBT two years ago.
17. Perhaps we can make the training instructor part of the task force team.
18. We can base the project in the Training Centre.
19. The Training department will still be in charge of training.
20. We'll promise to use the best bits from the existing courseware.
21. CBT investigation to be confined to sales training only.
22. CBT would not necessarily create a precedent. We could find that CBT isn't very good for things like business writing courses.
23. If the investigation is positive, we will pilot a trial CBT sales course and then we can all evaluate it afterwards.
24. A more effective training program might save Training from the chop during the recession.
25. We only need one head from Training initially, and he could be the redundant instructor.
26. We will provide some very experienced salesmen to help with the pilot.
27. We'll arrange for the Training Manager and the instructor to have their very own computer appreciation course.

There is no doubt that our case has now been considerably strengthened. We have a great deal more material than we had before we started this exercise. We may not use all of it, of course: the bit about 'a more effective training program might save Training from the chop' might not go down too well in a written report. Naturally, the negatives will be better expressed in a positive way, and all the new material will need to be woven into what we were already planning to say. Then the whole case will have to be organised and structured properly, as we shall see in the next chapter.

Incidentally, on our workshops we ask all attendees to bring along a real life case which is 'difficult' and 'important' for us to work through together. In every instance, using SCORE, STALL and FAILURE, they are able to think of at least one item under every heading, and sometimes as many as four or five.

FAILURE can be especially illuminating. Now and then – to their dismay – it uncovers an insoluble problem. Their original proposition is not viable in its current form, so they have to change it in some way. They tend to find that changing one or more of Aims, Action, or Audience usually solves the problem. They go for an objective which is less ambitious, or find another way to achieve it, or work through a different facilitator.

The exercise can also reveal that we have been using the wrong type of affinity. We may have been working on the basis that we had a Pleading Affinity, but if SCORE throws up some benefits (under Synergistic and Rewarding) which will appeal equally to the audience, perhaps we actually have a Selling Affinity. In turn, a Selling Affinity with benefits which apply to both author and audience should really be a Teamwork Affinity.

Interestingly, STALL and FAILURE can be used in reverse. Occasionally we all experience difficulty in making up our minds about buying something. We feel uneasy, but we can't put our finger on why. A useful trick is to imagine that the price had halved: if we still feel uneasy, then our hesitation is almost certainly due to a STALL or FAILURE problem. We can then apply the technique to identify our concern: we might be able to get something done about it. (For instance, if our problem is the gear stick, the car salesman might be prepared to throw in an automatic gearbox for nothing.)

SUMMARY

- Use SCORE to make the argument compelling
- List all the possible danger factors involved under the STALL and FAILURE headings
- Try to neutralise them by improving or expanding your argument
- If this is not possible, ask yourself seriously whether the proposition is really viable in its current form

9. Argument – Structuring

In the previous chapter, we saw how we could make our argument is compelling by making our proposition more attractive, and by anticipating and neutralising possible objections. In the next chapter, Appraisal, we shall be taking a cold look at the Argument as a whole and making some hard-nosed decisions about whether the communication will work in the way we intend it to. Before we can do that, we need to take all the various strands of our argument and weave them into a logical structure.

A colleague of Bryan's once failed to do this, and through a coincidental piece of misfortune, was obliged to take 'an unscheduled holiday'.

> *The marketing manager of one of our European subsidiaries had acquired an unhappy reputation for idleness.*
>
> *One year, he was asked to send his marketing plan to us at Head Office in advance of a top-level review meeting.*
>
> *When it arrived, it consisted of several hundred pages of text, graphs, and reporting charts. He had obviously made an effort this time, and his plan seemed to include a number of very good ideas. However, the whole thing was a mess. Sections were out of order, and there were some tables which didn't seem to relate to the text. When I tried to pull out his sales forecasts to go into my own presentation, I couldn't find them anywhere.*
>
> *I called him, and explained the problem. I waited while he fetched his own copy. After a long silence, he admitted he couldn't find the figures either. He was very apologetic. He explained that the plan*

had been produced under a great deal of pressure, and that he had dumped all his material on his secretary and asked her to put it together for him. She had obviously omitted the forecasts.

He promised to send me a revised version in time for the meeting. Meanwhile, would I please destroy the original?

A few days later, I called to check on progress, and to ask again for his sales forecasts. His office told me that, like two or three others, he had gone down with a serious bout of influenza.

So his plan was never reworked, and none of his efforts ever saw the light of day. When I came to cover his subsidiary at the review meeting, I explained as best I could that we hadn't received his final plan, and that he was flat on his back with 'flu. This was quite true, but to our Director, this sounded like the same old story. He shook his head sadly and said 'Situation normal . . .' A few knowing glances were exchanged among the others present.

I heard later that the unfortunate marketing manager had been fired soon afterwards.

When we prepare an argument, we usually find ourselves surrounded by evidence and opinions from various sources: notes from meetings and phone calls; memos and reports we asked for; extracts from published articles; tables of statistics, computer printouts, diagrams, photographs, maps . . . Even a completed SCORE, STALL and FAILURE form. This is just raw material. It is up to us to process it, and give it shape.

It might appear that structuring should be the last thing to do before we start to draft. In practice, however, much of the Appraisal section is to do with finding gaps and inconsistencies in our reasoning. Faults are easy to spot in a very short argument, but when we are trying to handle a complex piece of reasoning with a number of pieces of evidence, it's very difficult if we can't see the actual structure of our argument.

So we make a 'first pass' at ordering our material. Only then can we see whether we have the right facts, that we have drawn the right conclusions, or whether we may have missed something. If we find we need to make changes or additions, then we can introduce these into the structure of the argument and rearrange it again.

Outlining provides us with a discipline to do all this.

OUTLINING

Outlining means jotting down very simple key thoughts and organising them into a meaningful structure. When complete (and checked during Appraisal), the outline serves as the framework when we come to draft the argument in full. (We'll also find that the terse nature of the statements will be enormously helpful when we come to express our thoughts concisely and memorably, as we shall discuss under Articulation.)

Everybody who writes lengthy documents will normally start with some preliminary notes about structure and content, but most of us only take this process just so far. If time is short, we start writing what we hope and expect will be the final document. Only in the later stages do we find that we have omitted something, or that a critical part of the reasoning is in the wrong place.

Before the arrival of word processors, this used to be a major complication. Handwritten drafts would have whole chunks crossed out and little pieces of paper stapled to them with the insertions. And when the typed copy arrived, we found that the linking sentences and paragraphs no longer made sense, so back it went again for correction.

Although word processors now enable us to cut and paste large volumes of text, the basic difficulty still remains. The more we commit to the draft, the harder it becomes to reorganise and restructure later. Ideally, we should refrain from composing a single sentence until the outline is complete. Every five minutes spent outlining can save an hour's drafting.

SEQUENCING AND SUBORDINATION

Outlining does two things. It sets out the sequence or order in which the various points are to be expressed and it enables us to subordinate and relate thoughts one to another.

first topic
    first statement on first topic
    second statement on first topic

second topic
    first statement on second topic
        first discussion on first statement
        second discussion on first statement
    second statement on second topic
    third statement on second topic

third topic . . .

Many word processing packages include an outlining module for the very purpose, but the same result can be achieved by using tabs or indents in the normal editing mode. Items can be moved or promoted by using the usual 'move' or 'copy' commands.

If we don't have access to a word-processing system, we can still outline by hand on a sheet of paper. The insertion of arrows and/or numbers in the outline will usually be enough to make any reordering clear. (Bearing in mind that the idea is to use only very short phrases or sentences anyway, we can simply rewrite the whole thing if it becomes a bit of a tangle.)

There's also a little convention we use. We don't start sentences with capital letters. This avoids problems with proper names, and with the descriptive organisational labels which are so common in business. Since the statements are intentionally brief, there could be ambiguities:

Training is vital to the company.

This means that the company can't do without the Training department. If we meant that company personnel must have training, we would have used a small 't' at the beginning instead.

Now let's look over the Fuddle Sales Support Manager's shoulder to see how she could structure her material by using the outlining process. First, the ground covered during the meeting on Saturday. The notes she took probably look something like this:

Chris: we need to sharpen up in the recession.

Mike: pity the course was such a mess. (All: hear hear!)

Jerry had illegible handout copies on his course.

Role-playing brought up objections Robin couldn't handle.

Chris said CBT used in previous company (Banjax Ltd.) CBT lets you explore options, "what if"s.

Some customers would be put off by sales approach (Mike).

Chris said CBT would let you change it.

Sandy and Mike both lost orders while they were away on the course.

Viv: Damn traffic jams in the mornings.

Chris used to use CBT on the office PC in the evening.

Terry's course talked about selling dog food.

Steve's course was about selling "gizmos" (?)

Mike: course took too long.

Jim found it hard to keep up.

Chris: CBT lets you go back and revise.

Viv: we should be going for the affluent market.

Chris: Warning! Training Manager looked at CBT two years ago and thought it was silly.

Sales brochures are old (Steve).

In fact, the standard informal (chaotic?) meeting of Fuddle minds!

The Sales Support Manager knows she can't write this up just the way it stands:

Statements:	Syndromes
Chris: we need to sharpen up in the recession.	*need sales skills in the recession.*
Mike: pity the course was such a mess. (All: hear hear!)	*course not well received.*
Jerry had illegible handout copies on his course.	*poor handouts.*
Role-playing brought up objections Robin couldn't handle.	*weak on objections.*
Chris said CBT used in previous company (Banjax Ltd.). CBT lets you explore options, "what if"s.	*Banjax uses CBT! CBT allows students to explore options, "what if"s.*
Some customers would be put off by sales approach (Mike).	*suggested sales approach too aggressive.*
Chris said CBT would let you change it	*CBT allows customisation.*
Sandy and Mike both lost orders while they were away on the course.	*course attendance inconvenient.*
Viv: Damn traffic jams in the mornings.	*problems with getting to Training Centre.*
Chris used to use CBT on the office PC in the evening.	*CBT may be used anywhere, any time. CBT uses PCs.*
Terry's course talked about selling dog food.	*course not tailored to our products.*
Steve's course was about selling "gizmos" (?)	*courses seemed to vary in content.*
Mike: course took too long.	*course didn't cater for different learning abilities.*
Jim found it hard to keep up. Chris: CBT lets you go back and revise.	*CBT is student-paced.*
Viv: we should be going for the affluent market.	*target affluent market in the recession.*
Chris: Warning! Training Manager looked at CBT two years ago and thought it was silly.	*Training already rejected CBT.*

"We can't wait for the next instalment!"

The first thing she needs to do is to stop it sounding like the script for a soap. She can do this by taking the statements and turning them into facts or syndromes. That is, what do the comments really mean?

STRUCTURING THE OUTLINE

Next, she needs to impose some order on the various thoughts. The syndromes should be structured logically, with discussion about a topic in one place.

What do we mean by 'logical'? We can apply two useful techniques to the outline of an argument. Either can be an effective basic template for explaining a piece of reasoning.

Progressive format

The progressive format starts by stating what the discussion is about, then looks at some evidence, and finally ends with the key conclusion. Like a plot unfolding, in effect:

impact of recession.
    need to target affluent market
    therefore need sales skills
    therefore need training

The subject is 'impact of recession', and the conclusion is 'therefore need training'.

Declarative format

The declarative format is the other way round. We begin a discussion by stating a conclusion, and then follow it up with statements which support it:

current courses not highly regarded.
    seemed to vary in content (eg: dog food and gizmos).
    not tailored to our products.
    sales approach too aggressive.
    weak on handling objections.
    didn't cater for different abilities.
    poor handouts.
    attendance inconvenient (traffic jams).

The conclusion is 'course not highly regarded', and the following statements explain why.

Not only will these two formats help us get our thoughts together for the outline, but they will also make the task of expanding it into the final text considerably easier when we come to Articulation.

Now we can go back and fill in evidence and comment to the next level down. For instance, the Sales Support Manager recalls what Robin was saying about handling objections:

current courses not highly regarded.
    seemed to vary in content (eg: dog food and gizmos).
    not tailored to our products.
    sales approach too aggressive.
    weak on handling objections.

        subject not covered properly.
        only half a day given to it.
        problems with role-playing.
        instructor not much help.

    didn't cater for different abilities.
    poor handouts.
    attendance inconvenient (traffic jams).

Then she would go on and do the same for the other first level statements until the output from the meeting was covered.

Other evidence or related issues can then be introduced and added to the outline. For instance, she has a long list of things that SCORE, STALL and FAILURE made her think of, and these need to be worked into the outline too.

In this chapter, we have explained the principles of outlining. We'll produce the complete outline in the next chapter, Appraisal, when we shall be applying a few tests to see whether it will 'stand up in court', and also making a final decision about the method of delivery (meeting, phoning or writing).

SUMMARY

Build an outline of the intended argument as follows:

- Assemble relevant material
- Take each subject topic in order
- Express key points in short statements
- Use progressive or declarative formats to:
  - arrange them in sequence
  - relate them to each other.

10. Appraisal

There are three things which will persuade an audience.

1. **Trust in the author.**
2. **Sympathy with the proposition.**
3. **The reasoning behind the argument.**

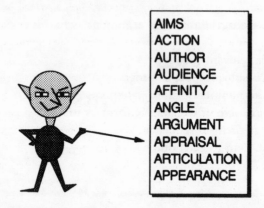

AIMS
ACTION
AUTHOR
AUDIENCE
AFFINITY
ANGLE
ARGUMENT
APPRAISAL
ARTICULATION
APPEARANCE

We have already covered the first two. We have explained the importance of choosing the right Author and presenting our credentials, and how to build a compelling proposition based upon SCORE, STALL and FAILURE. To some extent, either or both of these may well be enough. If the audience has total confidence in the author, they will accept an argument even if it's poorly presented. And if the proposition can be made extremely attractive, then approval will follow even if the author is unknown and the reasoning defective.

The problem arises when the audience has no particular reason to trust an Author, or when the proposition is in some way difficult or contentious. This situation is, of course, very common in business. The audience will then expect to see detailed and authoritative reasoning, especially if they foresee the need to justify their decision to others at some point. It's their head on the block as much as ours!

We used to have a director of international operations who was the scourge of his planning people. He would ruin presentation after presentation. During the technical sections, we would only nod, or offer encouraging comments such as 'Great . . .'. However, when the moment arrived for the financial projections, he would leap into action. He would seize upon numbers here and there, and politely ask what assumptions they were based on. The presenters would handle the inquisition as best they could, but there was always at least one assumption which seemed to have no pedigree. The meeting would be adjourned while someone was dispatched to go and find a father for it, or the presenters would withdraw en masse to 'rework the numbers'. Sometimes, they never came back!

When he retired, he had a farewell drink with a few of us. We ruefully congratulated him on his financial acuteness. He treated us to a wide smile, and admitted frankly that he rarely understood what the numbers really meant. He had simply discovered that the 'experts' always made one flaky assumption, and it was just a matter of time before he happened to point his finger at it. He felt he'd done his job if he forced us to check our assumptions again. (At this point, he took a beer mat and wrote the word ASSUME on it.)

'Otherwise', he explained, 'to ASSUME makes an ASS out of not only U, but ME too.'

Appraisal, then, covers the reasoning behind our argument. It appears on the 10A Form to remind us that we need to run through a checklist before we start drafting the argument. Any changes we make as a result are normally made to the outline set out under Argument.

A simple letter or memo will usually sail through the Appraisal without a hitch, but with anything complex or even faintly controversial, the Appraisal usually uncovers at least one gap in our reasoning. We might decide we ought to have a piece of evidence checked, or seek a second opinion on a particular matter. Sometimes we will need to go back to our experts and ask them to explain their conclusions again. We may trust their judgement, but why should we suppose our audience will do the same?

When we're sure the argument is watertight, we shall be making a final decision whether to meet, phone or write. We may have assumed we were writing a report, but if we unearth something very urgent, the audience is going to want to know why we didn't ring them right away.

APPRAISAL CHECKLIST

The checklist covers:

- Reasoning
- Ensuring accuracy
- Giving authority for evidence and conclusions
- Adding weight
- Presenting interested opinion
- Handling contradictory evidence and areas of doubt
- Making assumptions
- Covering alternative conclusions and recommendations
- Avoiding 'red rags'

Although the last point is not strictly part of the reasoning itself, we need to watch out for comments or statements which for one reason or another will annoy the audience. They will react emotionally, often to the point that any objective reasoning becomes fruitless!

REASONING

One of the first targets for attack will be the logic of our reasoning. Does the evidence point to the conclusions we have drawn? Have we made any sweeping statements?

The outlining process should have sidestepped major errors, but a frequent mistake is to jump to conclusions without apparently considering the evidence. We all do it, all the time. We become very attached to our own pet point of view, so unless the facts dramatically conflict with it, we tend to see what we want to see. Moreover, as we gain experience in business, we become energy-conscious: we like recycling earlier decisions. If the situation looks familiar, we use the same tried and tested solution without bothering to explain the reasoning.

In chapter 4, we said any communication will request or provide facts, interpretations, recommendations, or executive action.

It's useful if we imagine these arranged in a pyramid. The executive action or recommendations need to be supported by the interpretations, and these in turn must be firmly based upon the facts. If the bottom two layers are missing, our recommendations will seem like personal whims. Faulty exposition will endanger any kind of argument. We may well be absolutely right, but the audience needs to share our thinking. A sweeping statement such as 'Our products are uncompetitive' will need to be justified!

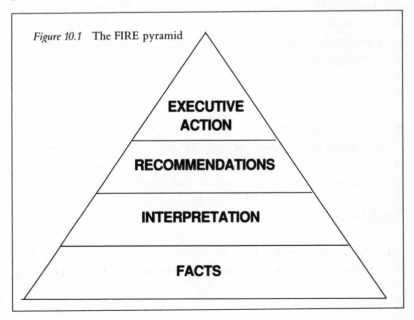

Figure 10.1 The FIRE pyramid

ACCURACY

We must get our facts right. The inaccuracies which usually slip through are those which seem to support our proposition. As authors, we welcome friendly evidence, so we are not inclined to question it. Unfortunately, our audience won't be so tolerant. If we complain that 'half of the July shipments were faulty', then the real figure had better not be 36 per cent.

Even if a mistake is an honest one, the audience will doubt not only our argument, but our motives. We must check facts, and state their credentials. If in doubt, we make sure that other parties will agree with our understanding and interpretation.

AUTHORITY

When looking at evidence and conclusions, our audience will be looking for authority. This means giving the sources of hard facts and opinion. So much the better if the sources are expert, disinterested and unanimous. Our proud claim that we now have 25 per cent of the market is best supported by plenty of evidence from published sources and independent agencies. Otherwise, it looks like a hopeful guess.

ADDING WEIGHT

Besides quoting authoritative sources, we can very often add weight to an argument by using 'precedents' and 'confessions'. If we can point to other instances where a similar argument was found to be valid, we should quote it. 'We came across this problem in France, and the measures we are proposing solved it on that occasion.'

If the audience has already agreed with at least part of the argument, this could be mentioned too. Salesmen use the 'confession' extensively. They try to gain our agreement as they lead us through their pitch. 'You agreed just now that you were looking for a high-yield investment. Why don't we take a look at our managed funds?'

PRESENTING INTERESTED OPINION

Many of our business judgements are based upon an opinion from other parties who may be well-informed, but who also have an interest in the outcome. Unfortunately, 'interest' usually suggests 'bias'. Audiences are guilty of faulty reasoning themselves from time to time. They assume that our supporters back our proposal because they are our supporters, rather than accept that they're our supporters because they agree with our proposal. This makes it tricky to demonstrate the extent of support we have from our constituents.

Suppose we in Marketing want the Financial Controller to agree to lower prices. We might start by quoting a knowledgeable authority:

The sales force says a price reduction is needed to boost sales . . .

"They would, wouldn't they? Anything for an easier life."

The authority is clearly 'interested'. To handle this, there are three basic strategies we can use, either separately or in combination.

First, we can play 'honest broker' by placing ourselves between the audience and the witness. We simply quote the points of view, declare the interest, and offer a judgement of our own:

Naturally, the sales force is screaming for a price reduction. I know we need to keep margins up, but I think they have a point.

This creates the impression of balance and even-handedness, as opposed to out-and-out interested lobbying.

Second, we could try a bit of name-dropping, citing a source which is trusted by the audience:

The Sales Director thinks a 15 per cent price reduction would be about right ...

We are now quoting a member of the same board tribe as the Controller, and a witness the Controller can't ignore.

Third, we can remind the audience of the Teamwork Affinity ('Let's work together to increase sales . . .'):

After all, our priority is revenue during these difficult times ...

As we know, a Teamwork Affinity is one which tends to avoid suspicion.

CONTRADICTORY EVIDENCE AND DOUBT

Although nobody expects a salesman to list the deficiencies in his product, our audience is justified in suspecting our argument if we suppress contradictory evidence or opinion.

Our excited claim that 'Research shows that the market is worth fifty million a year' is vulnerable if the sources disagree. It's more convincing to set out all the evidence and offer a considered judgement: 'The published report quoted twenty million, but our own consultants came up with fifty million. Since the latter estimate is based on more extensive fieldwork, it is likely to be more accurate.'

On the other hand, if we can't draw a reliable conclusion, we shouldn't try. Paradoxically, one of the most effective ways of lending our argument authority is to own up when we're not certain what the facts mean, or what to do about them. This gives us more credibility on the occasions when we say we really are sure.

Admittedly the expression of doubt requires a strong stomach, especially when dealing with some top executives who feel they have to make mission-critical decisions on a production-line basis. To them, doubt smells like indecisiveness, but in the long run a delayed decision is better than a wrong one.

One possible strategy is to set out what we plan to do to resolve the doubt: 'We will need to commission further research before we finally make a commitment to the plan . . .'

ASSUMPTIONS

A very quick way to destroy the authority of our statements is to make unwarranted assumptions. All arguments are based upon assumptions. Some are so obvious that nobody feels the need to state them. 'Assuming we're all still in business next week . . .' is a reasonable basis on which to work.

One important set of assumptions are those we make when presenting financial projections. We build an impressive business plan with forecasts of revenue, profit, market share and so on, but our calculations are based upon assumptions of, for example, market sizes, growth rates, interest rates, unit costs . . . Somehow, somewhere, we must mention what these assumptions are.

If they are 'company standards', we say so. (We may not believe them, but now is not the time to start a long debate about how the organisation calculates its standard costs, or where in the accounting chain the company wants to take its profit. We play by the rules. If they need changing, we can take up that battle another day.)

Aside from numbers, there may be some assumptions we made ourselves. Our new business plan may assume that the increase in sales can be handled by the existing sales force, or that our suppliers can increase output to meet demand. Hidden assumptions like these will quickly sprout into linkage, risk, or uncertainty problems if we're not careful. We'll need some authority to support these assumptions if the whole argument is not to crash around our ears.

ALTERNATIVES

The audience needs to feel confident that we have explored all the options. When we're looking at a problem methodically, we usually work through a series of possible solutions until we find the best fit. Or if time is short, we may seize upon the first solution which occurs to us, perhaps one kindly donated by our supporters. Both situations contain dangers.

If we have tried and discarded a number of potential solutions, we need to expose our thinking to the audience. In a live discussion, they will prompt us with 'Did you consider Swindon for the relocation as well? Or did you just pick Milton Keynes because you live there?' But they can't do this when we're writing. It's wise to cover the alternatives and give some indication that they have been closely examined and found wanting.

If, on the other hand, we arrived at the answer in one move, we should pause and think whether there might be some other less-obvious but better solution. Our aims will help. What are we trying to achieve? And is our answer the best or only one? If we don't think of all the options, someone else will.

RED RAGS

It's a wise move to have our final draft checked by someone else in case we have accidentally included something which will upset our audience. However, it's also prudent to do a check ourselves during the appraisal process before something controversial becomes inextricably woven into the argument.

The commonest red rags are challenges to Theology (as discussed under STALL in chapter 8) so we should have eliminated them by now. However, they also include statements which imply criticism or which remind the audience of some unpleasant experience. For instance, 'We must avoid the sort of fiasco we had in Spain last year' is best omitted, especially if our audience happens to include the Spanish General Manager at the time!

If we need the reference as evidence, we must take care not to apportion blame. 'The new marketing initiative failed to meet its targets' is less of a red rag than 'the Marketing Director screwed up . . .'

THE FUDDLE ARGUMENT

To show how to carry out a complete Appraisal, let's take the argument we were outlining in the last chapter.

1. **Aims (operational objective)**
   improve sales training.
2. **Action (desired effect of the communication)**
   Training to agree to look again at CBT.
3. **Author (sender of the communication)**
   sales director. tribe = Fuddle. aims = increase sales/
   effective sales force/improve sales training.
4. **Audience (recipients of the communication)**
   personnel director/training manager. tribe = Fuddle.
   aims = effective sales training/improve sales
   training.
5. **Affinity (relationship between author and audience)**
   teamwork: "Let's both look again at CBT as a
   possible solution."
6. **Angle (point of view to be adopted)**
   shared.
7. **Argument (supporting reasoning)**

Since the Argument section in this case is quite long, we would have to use an extra sheet:

Argument:

   impact of recession.
     need to target affluent market.
     therefore need sales skills.
     therefore training important.

current courses not highly regarded.
   seemed to vary in content (eg: dog food and gizmos).
   not tailored to our products.
      attendees couldn't relate to dog food/gizmos.
   sales approach too aggressive.
weak on handling objections.
   subject not covered properly.
      only half a day given to it.
   problems with role-playing.
      instructor not much help.
didn't cater for different abilities.
poor handouts.
attendance inconvenient (traffic jams).

CBT has advantages.
   uses PCs (might need memory upgrade).
same courseware for all.
   can avoid differences from course to course.
   unaffected by change of instructor.
customisable to our products.
   easier to concentrate on sales process.
   can be upgraded as new products introduced.
student-paced.
   current training moves at pace of the slowest.
good for revision, and exploring options.
   students prefer to ask machine to repeat parts.
can be used any time, anywhere.
   doesn't interfere with normal daily tasks.
   emergencies can be dealt with.
other companies using it.
   Banjax already using it successfully.

recommend setting up investigation team.
   CBT could be used for other types of training too.
      but no good for things like "Business Writing".
      so investigation for sales training only.

joint task force with Training, IT and Sales.
   Sales will do the hard work.
   only one body needed from Training.
     no impact on Training's schedules.
   task force now a very common approach.
     good for multi-discipline projects.
     breaks down barriers, improves relations.
   base the project in the Training Centre.
   Sales to get cooperation IT on technical issues.
   computer appreciation course for Training people?

if investigation positive, pilot sales CBT program.
   decide details later.
   joint approach to secure pilot funding.
   use best bits from the existing courseware.
   Sales to provide experienced salesmen to help.
   joint evaluation afterwards.
   Training will still be in charge of training.
     Training to take credit for introducing CBT.
   opportunity for Fuddle to be in forefront.

Now let's place it under the microscope . . .

OUR REASONING

Where are the flaws? As it happens, there aren't too many, since the very process of outlining forced us to order the argument logically.
   But here's one, right at the beginning:

   impact of recession.
✗   need to target affluent market.
   therefore need sales skills.
   therefore need training.

We have built our reasoning on the 'need to target the affluent market'. So far as we know, not even the Sales Director has agreed to this strategy, let alone any of the other directors. This is asking for trouble. In any event, we still need training whatever market segments we're going for. So we change that to:

impact of recession.
   need to be competitive.
   therefore need sales skills.
   therefore need training.

Here's a couple more in the section about the advantages of CBT:

CBT has advantages.
     uses PCs (might need memory upgrade).
   same courseware for all.
     can avoid differences from course to course.
     unaffected by change of instructor.
✗   customisable to our products.
     easier to concentrate on sales process.
     can be upgraded as new products introduced.
   student-paced.
     can cater for extremes of ability.
   good for revision, and exploring options.
     students prefer to ask machine to repeat parts.
✗   can be used any time, anywhere.
     doesn't interfere with normal daily tasks.
     emergencies can be dealt with.
   other companies using it.
     Banjax already using it successfully.

The idea that CBT can be customised to our own products may be true, but that's not an advantage peculiar to CBT. There's no reason why the current training courses couldn't have included our own products instead of dog food. The idea is simply in the wrong place. It needs to come later, when we're discussing a pilot CBT programme.

A claim is made that it 'can be used any time, anywhere': since it uses the office PCs, it doesn't follow we can take the thing home, or that it won't interfere with anybody wanting to use the machine for sales prospecting. So we change that to:

> *any time during office hours.*
>   *doesn't interfere with normal sales activity.*

Finally, in the section when we're discussing the pilot:

  if investigation positive, pilot sales CBT program.
    decide details later.
    joint approach to secure pilot funding.
✗   use best bits from the existing courseware.
    Sales to provide experienced salesmen to help.
    joint evaluation afterwards.
    Training will still be in charge of training.
      Training to take credit for introducing CBT.
    opportunity for Fuddle to be in forefront.

The two training techniques are different, so we may not be able to use any of it at all. So:

> *try to use best bits from the existing courseware.*

ACCURACY

Are there any inaccuracies? There may be one in the section criticising the courses:

  current courses not highly regarded.
    seemed to vary in content (eg: dog food and gizmos).
    not tailored to our products.
      attendees couldn't relate to dog food/gizmos.
    sales approach too aggressive.

weak on handling objections.
subject not covered properly.
only half a day given to it.
problems with role-playing.
instructor not much help.
didn't cater for different abilities.
poor handouts.
attendance inconvenient (traffic jams).

Were the poor handouts a general problem? A few quick calls reveal that it was an isolated instance. On the last day of one of the courses, the copier broke down. However, the instructor stayed late that evening and did the handouts again. The attendees had clean copies on their desks by the following Monday morning. We have just avoided antagonising our audience unnecessarily, and the predictable response:

"Do you people have it in for us, by any chance?"

AUTHORITY

What can we do to beef up the authority of our statements?

We should use the before and after sales figures as hard evidence, and quote Accounts as the disinterested source.

We could also make a note to attach some press articles on the benefits of current CBT systems.

ADDED WEIGHT

We have some precedents: we can point to Banjax and other cases from the press articles. We also have something of a confession. We might quote the earlier memo from the Personnel Director which admits there is a problem with current training. And getting the figures from Accounts was suggested by the Personnel Director himself.

INTERESTED OPINION

Do we have any interested opinion, and if so, how will we handle it? The criticisms about the current course and the benefits of CBT may all be interpreted as interested opinion. The information about the latest CBT systems is from *CBT Monthly,* which may well be applying a liberal dose of hype. The Sales Director himself (the ostensible Author) can't really underwrite the opinion, simply because he wasn't on the courses and isn't a CBT expert.

So we had better play honest broker. We could introduce the section on the current courses with:

> *current training.*
> > *attendees say current courses not highly regarded.*
> > > *genuinely held opinions, and unanimous.*

And start the section about CBT with:

> *claimed advantages of CBT.*
> > *based on published articles.*
> > > *may be overstated.*
> > *but supported by experience of one of our salesmen.*

CONTRADICTORY EVIDENCE OR DOUBT

While we have no contradictory evidence, we do have areas of doubt, mainly the claims made for CBT. So how will we resolve that doubt? We can change the beginning of the section on setting up an investigation team to read:

> *recommend setting up investigation team.*
> > *need to check out effectiveness in practice first.*
> > *contact other CBT users.*
> > *possibly also use consultants to research satisfaction.*
> *(etc . . .)*

ASSUMPTIONS

There are two assumptions in the section where we discuss the investigation team:

> recommend setting up investigation team.
> ...
> ✗   base the project in the Training Centre.
> ✗   Sales to get cooperation from IT on technical issues.
> computer appreciation course for Training people?

A minor point, but unless we want to start a long debate about whether there is room in the Centre or not, we'll change that to:

> *base the project in the Training Centre if possible.*

The assumption about IT might be tricky:

"Suppose they don't want to know?"

We had better have a Plan B up our sleeve:

> Sales to get cooperation IT on technical issues
> *or use outside CBT consultant.*

When going through an appraisal, we may find only a few faults in our reasoning. However, we almost always discover that we have left a host of assumptions lying about to trip us up. We won't labour the point with the Fuddle argument, but here's just a few more which spring to mind without much effort:

- We assumed that the dissatisfied attendees did their course pre-work properly. If they hadn't, we can hardly complain about the courses.
- We assumed that the Sales Director has never formally reviewed the course and given his approval. If he has, then this could be embarrassing. (We might find his 'confession' being used against us!
- We assumed that the Banjax CBT system was successful. Chris only said that they used it. Perhaps it was a horrendous shambles to begin with . . .

All these things are easy assumptions to make, but they need to be checked.

ALTERNATIVES

At the beginning of the argument, we plan to talk about the impact of the recession, and then say that in order to be competitive, we need good training:

```
  impact of recession.
✗    need to be competitive.
     therefore need sales skills.
     therefore need training.
```

A quick-thinking audience might be wondering what else we're doing to become more competitive. Are there other options? Of course. So we need to explain these, just to be on the safe side. We might, therefore, change the introduction completely to read:

```
  impact of recession.
    need to be competitive.
    measures being taken:
      price reduction.
      product improvements.
      new announcement imminent.
```

sales skills needed to make the most of these.
therefore training important.

What about the proposition itself?

"OK. So why don't we just rework the course?"

From the point of view of the audience, CBT is not the only solution which might improve sales training. As we know, that's not what they had in mind at all. Therefore, we need to show that we have thought about it, and that we have weighed the pros and cons. We can do this by adding a new section before we discuss CBT:

> *options.*
> *revise current courses.*
> *purchase new course from provider.*
> *subcontract sales training altogether.*
> *computer-based training.*

RED RAGS

The main potential source of irritation is the fact that Training have already looked at CBT and dismissed it. This needs careful handling. We should avoid any hint of criticism, and give reasons why the decision should be reconsidered. Something like this needs to go in:

> CBT already investigated and rejected by Training.
> possibly with justification.
> but CBT probably improved since then.
> only option which doesn't take salesmen out of the field.

Delete the fact that the instructor was not much help during the role-playing. It's sufficient to blame the courseware. We don't have to lynch the instructor too.

Finally, a relatively minor one:

attendance inconvenient (traffic jams).

Pulling salesmen off the job to attend a course is one thing, but mentioning the morning traffic will not attract much sympathy from Training who have to sit in it every day! The point sounds petty anyway, so we leave it out.

Meet, phone or write decision

We think we're writing a report. Are we still sure about that? In chapter 2 we showed a very simple decision matrix which gives a quick guide to which method to use to communicate our message.

Which of the following apply to the Fuddle argument?

		M	P	W
No	Long distance?		√	√
No	One-to-many?	√		√
No	One-to-very many?			√
Yes	Show commitment?	√	√	
No	Seeking clarification?	√	√	
No	Discuss and explore?	√	√	
No	Urgent answer needed?	√	√	
Yes!	Considered response needed?			√
Yes	Complex argument?			√
Yes	Visible evidence?	√		√
No	Audible/tangible evidence?	√		
No	Language problems?			√
Yes	Permanent record?			√
No	Off-the-record?	√	√	

Simply flushing out the 'No's' leaves us with:

		M	P	W
Yes	Show commitment?	√	√	
Yes!	Considered response needed?			√
Yes	Complex argument?			√
Yes	Visible evidence?	√		√
Yes	Permanent record?			√

Our conclusion? Yes, it will have to be a written proposal, but we could do with a meeting or a phone call to back it up, and to register the importance we attach to it.

So what's left? The 10A Technique has helped the Sales Support Manager build and expand the communication into something even the Sales Director is not expecting to put his name to. Since he is the nominal Author, it would be a good idea for her to check the various points of the outline with him first, and agree how the message will be delivered.

He agrees. The idea now is to send copies of the proposal to the Personnel Director and the Training Manager, and ask for a meeting to discuss it.

But first, she has to write it! She'll shortly be taking some fresh paper, or keying the outline into her word-processor to start drafting. But before then, there are some things she'll need to consider which will affect how she structures the communication, the way she uses words and figures, and the final appearance of the document. These issues are discussed in the next three chapters.

SUMMARY

- Use the FIRE pyramid to make sure:
  - you have the Facts
  - which support your Interpretation
  - which supports your Recommendation or Executive Action
- Check facts for accuracy
- Give sources for evidence and opinion
- Add weight with:
  - precedents
  - confessions
- Present interested opinion by:
  - playing 'honest broker'
  - citing acceptable sources
  - underlining a Teamwork Affinity
- Don't suppress contradictory evidence or genuine doubt
- Check and state assumptions
- Include and discuss all the alternatives
- Look out for red rags
- Reconsider any decision to meet, phone or write

And now might be a good time to make a copy of the 10A Form with your persuasive argument on it before someone accidentally junks it!

11. Articulation – Words

Up to this point, we have been concentrating on building our message and preparing an outline of our Argument. Articulation covers the way we express it, and it covers both document structure and language.

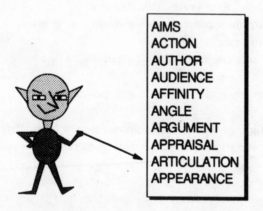

AIMS
ACTION
AUTHOR
AUDIENCE
AFFINITY
ANGLE
ARGUMENT
APPRAISAL
ARTICULATION
APPEARANCE

Jim and his planning people had decided that a particular programme should be put out to tender to a number of software houses. They drew up a shortlist, and Jim added the name of a programmer – Eddie – whom he had known from his previous company. Eddie was extremely skilled and had built up a reputation for work of top quality before setting up in business with a few of his cronies.

Jim invited Eddie to call. He explained that they wanted written proposals, and that these would be evaluated by a committee of five.

They would be looking specifically for statements about costs and timescales, and for evidence that the requirements were understood. If his proposal was successful, a detailed specification and contract would follow.

Eddie's proposals arrived. They consisted of thirty pages of chaotic typewritten text. There were no paragraphs, sentences rambled on interminably, and the language was complicated and obscure. As far as Jim could make out, about half of the document was devoted to Eddie's past successes, and the rest described the techniques Eddie would be using to write the programme. Jim couldn't see anything about the requirement, but he did eventually discover a throw-away sentence about costs and timescales half-way down page 26.

At the committee meeting, Eddie's proposal was rejected out of hand. Apart from Jim, none had bothered to read it. They said they hadn't had time to wade through and find what they had asked for.

Jim couldn't complain about the decision.

Neither could Eddie.

COMMUNICATING TO PERSUADE

The premise of *Manage the Message* is that we communicate to achieve an objective through persuasion, so we shall be concentrating on ways to make our message both understandable and memorable. We won't be too concerned about 'incorrect' structures, style, phraseology, grammar, spelling or punctuation, unless they get in the way. The techniques we shall be describing won't win any prizes for literature, but they'll help put our message across and create the right impression with the minimum of effort.

JERKS

While we're doing this, we'll be keeping a lookout for 'jerks'. A jerk is anything which will distract the audience from the process of absorbing the message. A jerk can be, for instance, a sudden shift of direction in the reasoning, an abrupt change of style, an ambiguity or a misused word. Jerks cause the audience to lose the train of thought, to misunderstand, become annoyed, or howl with laughter when they're supposed to be impressed. Jerks are something we can definitely do without.

COMMUNICATING TO INFORM

A word of warning, however. There will be occasions when we are communicating to inform, rather than to motivate. Although our suggestions will make our communication clear and easy to assimilate, a few of them could well irritate an audience which is just expecting an exposition of the facts. For instance, this chapter explains – among other things – how to use structure to highlight conclusions and recommendations. This is fine when we are putting a point of view to the audience, but the effect might seem presumptuous to another audience: their reaction could be 'You provide the facts, and I'll decide what they mean!'

There are other books which explain in detail how to write technical or straightforward factual reports, and it's not our intention to reinvent that particular wheel. However, for safety's sake, we shall be pointing out where our suggestions might be counter-productive in such situations.

USER-FRIENDLINESS

Generally, our aim is to make our persuasive message user-friendly.

In order to judge user-friendliness we need to understand how the audience will actually use the communication. Most of the special problems involved with writing arise from the fact that we do not receive any feedback from our audience as they read it. We therefore have to use our imagination.

It's a natural mistake to assume that the audience will devote the same amount of time and attention to reading the document that the writer put into composing it. Like the cook who sees his guests spend fifteen minutes swallowing the meal that took three hours to prepare, many authors would be horrified to see the treatment their creation receives in practice.

Our envelope arrives with a stack of others. The first question the audience asks is 'Is this really for me?', closely followed by 'Who's it from?' and 'What's it about?' Then, 'Do I tackle this now, or can it wait?' The letterhead, addressee and the subject are usually enough for this decision.

When the audience reads it, they first look for some clue as to what the communication is asking them to do, and why. This usually involves scanning the first paragraph, glancing at the odd point in the middle, and then straight to the end. Then maybe back again.

If they are still interested, they will start skip-reading, sampling the beginning (and sometimes ending) of various paragraphs to get a feel for the argument, and peeking at any graphs, tables or photographs. Only if they alight on something they didn't expect or understand will they read all the words in between. Once. And then with some impatience. If they still can't get the meaning, they won't bother.

How do we make our written communication user-friendly? We have a number of useful tips to consider. These cover:

- Attracting attention
- Making navigation easy
- Expanding the outline into something understandable
- Making the text easy to read
- Choosing memorable expressions
- Using humour

ATTRACTING ATTENTION

We probably have about 10 seconds to 'hook' a busy audience and give them a reason to read the communication. With the Fuddle report, a beginning like this won't do the trick:

Advantages of CBT

Although introduced some years ago, CBT has taken some time to be accepted as a means of industrial training. Early

62

problems with hardware and software tended to discourage potential users . . .

The Personnel Director may gather it's something to do with training, so he might scribble 'Yours, I think' on the top and bat it off to the Training Manager.

This would be better:

Report on Fuddle Sales Training

In this report, we assess the effectiveness of the company's current sales training, and make recommendations for improving it. The issue has become very important to the company because the sales force needs to operate at peak productivity in the current recession.

Within a few seconds, he can see that it's about the company sales training, that there are some recommendations, and that the issue is very important to the company right now. As the board member with ultimate responsibility for training, this concerns him.

What will he do next? He'll probably skim through, trying to understand the gist of it, and what he is supposed to do. How can we help him find his way through the report?

NAVIGATION

Structure is critical. If there is no structure, and points are being picked up and dropped at random, the reader will assume that the author's mind is in a similarly confused state. The outlining process should have avoided this sort of mess, but logical ordering is only half the job. We need to put up plenty of flags and signposts to catch the reader's eye and direct his or her attention.

Structures can be informal or formal. Formal structures have separate sections with their own labels attached in the form of headings, while informal structures are less explicitly laid out.

FORMAL STRUCTURES

A formal structure is required if the document is long and complex. A comprehensive report or brief with detailed evidence and reasoning needs an explicit framework, with a table of contents, numbered section headings, appendices and so on.

Some organisations have standards for formal report structures, so unless we want to jerk the reader before he's even read a single word, it's wise to observe them. Most, however, don't, and the writer is left to his or her own devices.

So here are some suggestions.

COMPLEX REPORTS

Let's assume a worst case: a detailed report on the relative merits of Czechoslovakia, Hungary and Poland as the next phase in our plan to conquer the world. It will have a wide readership, and is intended as an internal reference document. The length will probably be in excess of twenty pages, and may go to over a hundred.

The overall structure might look like this:

- Title page, with:
  subject
  distribution list
  author
  date
  revision level.

- Disclaimers and acknowledgements, if any

- Table of contents

- Main body of report (*see below*)

- Appendices, with:
  tables
  graphs
  references.

And, if we really want to go the whole way:

- Glossary
- Index.

The main body of the report would then be laid out like this:

1. Objectives, terms of reference
2. Executive summary, with:
   conclusions
   recommendations
   key assumptions.

(This is as far as many readers will go!)

3. Introduction and background
   (including any previous history)
4. Case # 1 (e.g., Czechoslovakia)
   Detailed exposition, including facts, interpretations, options, recommendations, assumptions
5. Case # 2 (e.g., Hungary)
   (*ditto . . .*)
6. Case # 3 (e.g., Poland)
   (*ditto . . .*)
7. Conclusions and recommendations.

This, of course, is a complex case, and the audience will appreciate all the help we can give with navigation, including numbered and headed subsections within the main sections.

SIMPLE REPORTS

For a shorter report, the structure needs to be simplified, with some of the sections combined into one. Having numbered sections containing only one short sentence is perhaps too formalised.

The Fuddle report, for instance, will probably be five or six pages in length. In this case, the structure can be very flexible, but should roughly follow the same progression as the complex structure shown above:

- Simple title page, with:
    subject
    author
    date.

(That's if we're not bothered about BS 5750. Otherwise, it's something like we showed for the complex report above.)

1. Introduction, with;
     objectives, scope, background, etc.

2. Executive summary, with
     brief conclusions, recommendations.

3. The problem or opportunity

4. Options

5. Recommendations

6. Summary, including:
     action plan, if any.

- Appendix, with:
    any supporting evidence.

COVERING LETTERS

Should we send the report on its own? Probably not. A covering letter is a good idea when:

- We suspect the audience may not even read the executive summary
- We want to reinforce the conclusions
- Copies of the communication are to be sent to different readers for different purposes. (We need to customise the 'hooks')
- Passing on something written by someone else

For the Fuddle report, a covering letter might solve the problem about where to put the 'confession', that is, a reference to the fact that Personnel already accept the need to change the current courses. Bearing in mind that the report could well have a wider circulation than Personnel (it might come in useful to brief the IT department, among others) putting this in a covering letter might be appreciated by the Personnel Director.

We might also think about an advance letter (or phone call) while we're producing the report. This is advisable when:

- We're running late with the communication
- The conclusions or recommendations are urgent and totally unexpected (spectacularly good or bad)
- We want the recipient to give it special treatment

INFORMAL STRUCTURES

While formal structures are vital with long reports, a short memo or letter can simply follow a logical train of thought.

From: the Managing Director
To: Administration Director

During fire alarm practice on Wednesday last, a number of personnel failed to go to the assembly area. Can you please tell me how many stayed in their offices, and why? This is a very serious matter, and I would like your suggestions on how we can ensure that everybody vacates the building in future.

This is clear enough. Indeed, a formal structure for such a note will seem oddly over-emphatic:

1. During fire alarm practice on Wednesday last, a number of personnel failed to go to the assembly area.
2. Can you please tell me how many stayed in their offices?
3. Why?
4. This is a very serious matter, and I would like your suggestions on how we can ensure that everybody vacates the building in future.

"What else does this character do by numbers?"

The response could well be:

From: Administration Director
To: the Managing Director

1. I know.
2. 17.
3. They did not hear it.
4. Noted.

Quite apart from short letters, a formal structure may not always be appropriate even for some types of longer document. An obvious example is a sales letter, when we're trying to be informal. We still need a structure, so we have to work harder with sequencing, linking and signposting. This is where the expansion of our outline can help.

EXPANDING THE OUTLINE

At this point, we may have added some new section headings to our outline, and made a note that we shall need an executive summary, for instance. Alternatively, we have decided on a completely informal structure. Either way, we can now make a start on turning the little outline statements into something our audience will understand. This involves both expansion and linking. The development of the text should be logical and smooth, with thoughts clearly related to each other. If we structured our outline properly, we should find that the whole thing falls neatly into place:

```
background.
    measures being taken:
        price reduction.
        product improvements.
        new announcement imminent.
    sales force needs sales skills to make the most of these.
    therefore training important.
```

This would become something like:

Background

As you know, the company has taken a number of urgent steps to improve our competitive position during the recession. We have recently introduced very keen pricing structures, and a number of improvements have been made to our current product range. We shall announce an important new product in a few weeks.

In order for us to reap maximum benefit from these moves, our sales force needs to work at high levels of competence. They should therefore have the best sales training that we can provide.

All the points are in there, and it's now in English. Our skip-reading audience will be able to pick on the opening key sentence (about urgent steps to improve our competitive position) and then jump to the final sentence which carries the conclusion (the need for sales training). They may ignore the bits in between, but they have collected the gist of our message before they move on.

BEWARE DIVERSIONS

When expanding the outline, we often find a different way of saying something. In the above example, 'therefore training important' became 'They should therefore have the best sales training that we can provide.' This is normal, and a good thing, since it allows us to use our imagination. However, it's easy to become sidetracked as more points occur to us. While there's no harm in filling out the reasoning, a major diversion into another subject is a clear jerk.

For example, this piece of outline:

```
what is CBT?
  uses PCs.
  might need memory upgrade. (+ CBT Monthly)
```

. . . might turn into this:

Computer-based training

CBT uses personal computers (PCs) to run the training program. Our own PCs might need more memory, but otherwise standard machines can be used. (A more detailed technical explanation is given in the attached article from CBT Monthly.) *Some systems use interactive video to teach students how to dismantle car engines, for instance, and can show where all the nuts are. We believe a videodisc is needed for this.*

"We already know where the nuts are!"

Thinking about the magazine article reminded us of something we read there about interactive videodisc, so we slipped it in as a bit of background. However, we have now dragged the audience off on to a sidetrack which is irrelevant to the report.

AMBIGUITIES

Sometimes, the diversion can be completely unintentional. Certain words are ambiguous in themselves. 'While', for instance, often causes problems, since it can mean 'although' and 'for as long as':

While our targets are not being met . . .

After reading the first seven words, the audience might have been expecting something like:

. . . sales have nevertheless showed an encouraging upward trend.

But suppose the rest of the sentence were:

. . . we must make every effort to contain expenses . . .

This would be a jerk. The safe thing to do is to use 'although' when this is what we mean.

Jerks can also occur when we use words which can be nouns, adjectives or verbs. One sentence opening which recently caused us a double-take was:

The job cuts across the company . . .

Having read that, we were anticipating something like:

. . . will cause hardship for employees.

But the rest of it was actually:

. . . policy for employees nearing retirement age.

An audience bent on absorbing the message as quickly as possible will be irritated by this kind of jerk because they are forced to re-read the sentence. Or it could be that, having taken in the opening words, they have formed a mistaken impression of what the sentence is about, and then moved on before they realise the intended meaning.

Finally, we must keep a sharp lookout for the ambiguity which results from a misplaced phrase or sentence:

North Region continues to fall behind. While North Region sales have been running nearly 10 per cent below last year's, Southern Region is 22 per cent up. I recommend we take immediate steps to rectify this situation.

We can't have Southern doing that, now can we?

ENCAPSULATION

If we have followed the outlining discipline rigorously, we should find that we can encapsulate a discussion on a particular topic in one or more successive paragraphs. This is exactly what the reader will expect. However, when we're referring to another point discussed elsewhere in the text, it's tempting to tell the audience to go and fetch it themselves:

CBT is student-paced, and avoids the problems described in section 5 above. It allows each student to work at the speed most suitable for him or her.

This is another type of "jerk", and a very exasperating one. The reader has to go back and re-read the section referred to. It's even worse when the referral is forwards: the audience might forget to return afterwards.

Even though it will result in having to use more words, the safe thing to do is restate the conclusion instead of referring back:

CBT is student-paced. *As we have seen, traditional classroom-based teaching methods have difficulty in matching the speed of the course to varying levels of ability.* CBT allows each student to work at the speed most suitable for him or her.

PARAGRAPHING

Back in the mists of time, we can all dimly recall being taught rules about paragraphs. However, any rules now seem to be 'more honoured in the breach than the observance'. We have seen pieces of complex reasoning with paragraphs which go on for pages at a stretch. At the same time, the leader writer in our local newspaper insists on giving every single sentence its own paragraph.

A working rule is to break a paragraph when there is a noticeable change in the subject matter, but never to let one go on for more than, say, five or six sentences. This is about as much as the audience's eye and brain can take before demanding a break.

An exception is when we want to highlight an important sentence. If we make it a paragraph of its own, it will attract the eye of the skip reader.

Following the simple techniques we have just described will set a firm framework for the content of our communication. Now we are ready to think about style and phraseology, starting with readability.

READABILITY

The factors which affect readability are:

- The length and familiarity of the words
- The length and complexity of sentences
- The simplicity and directness of expression

As always, these things should be considered from the audience's point of view. Some individuals have a strong grasp of vocabulary and grammar, and like to keep their verbal physique in good trim.

Their audiences may be of a similar mind and they can happily work out together. However, this is not normally the case in business: the reader wants to get at the meaning, and quickly.

A very common delusion is that long words and sentences somehow impress, and sound authoritative and businesslike. They don't: for most audiences, they just make reading and understanding that much harder.

No matter how much effort we have put into the argument, any meaning we may have intended will be obscured by the use of long and complicated sentences and unfamiliar words, and we may also attract a certain amount of ridicule.

FOG INDEXING

A useful objective measurement of "readability" is Gunning's Fog Index. Although it has been around for some decades now, it's a useful guide, and we often use it to check our own writing style from time to time. There are variations on the original, but the version we use works like this:

1. Take a piece of text of at least 100 words.
2. Count the number of words in the text.
3. Count the number of sentences.
4. Divide the total words by the total sentences. This gives the average sentence length.
5. Count the number of words with three or more syllables.
6. Express this is a percentage of the total words (from 2).
7. Fog index is (4) plus (6).

THICKENERS

A moment's thought will show that the following will increase the 'fogginess' of our text:

- Long sentences
- Many conditional clauses
- Long words, especially those of Latin or Greek origin

171

(Examples are those ending in '. . . ance', '. . . ation', '. . . ition', or '. . . ology' and their derivatives. 'Significance', 'realisation', 'institutional', 'tautologically' and so on.)

THINNERS

Conversely, these tend to clear the fog:

- Short sentences
- Few clauses
- Short words, especially Anglo–Saxon words

In practice, fog indexes can range from about 5 (for a children's pre-reader) to over 60 for a complicated technical description. (The average for this book, by the way, is around 30.)

While the total fog index itself is a useful guide, we can also make a separate note of the two components, the average sentence length and the percentage of long words, since these can show us where we're going wrong.

Let's have a look at some real-life examples:

Example 1

This is taken from a short story, written in the first person:

> By the afternoon, I was beginning to regret I'd taken the job. The rain was falling more heavily, and the east wind was penetrating my anorak as I lay full length in the grass.
>
> I shivered and raised my head. The house, a good three hundred yards away down the slope, still appeared deserted. I'd had the place in full view since daybreak, and there had been no sign of life at all.
>
> I glanced at my watch. Three-thirty. It would be dark soon, and then the long lens on the Canon would be useless anyway. I wondered whether the whole thing had gone wrong somewhere along the line. Perhaps they'd had trouble with the car. Or maybe the girlfriend had just changed her mind . . .

This is part of a piece of text we tested, and the fog index was 17. This is very low for adult reading, and ideal for light fiction. The style is conversational. Sentences are reasonably short with very few subsidiary clauses, giving an average sentence length of 12.6.

The main reason for the low index, however, is that it contains very simple words. It is helped by the fact that much of the description is of a physical nature, rather than abstract. English has a wealth of short punchy words for everyday objects and events: 'rain', 'wind', 'grass', 'head', 'house' and so on. (All the things our Saxon ancestors used to worry about.) Abstract terms, on the other hand, tend to be of Latin or Greek origin, and as we shall see, they will increase the index.

Examples 2 and 3

These are actual reports from two different newspapers a little while ago. They cover similar subjects:

> *Drastic retail price rises for food and consumer goods will be introduced in the Soviet Union in the next few months.*
>
> *The rises follow huge increases in the energy, raw materials and engineering equipment bills facing all Soviet enterprises.*
>
> *The announcement yesterday was however tempered with the promise that the government measures would include automatic compensation for the price rises in pensions, wages and allowances.*

> *Chancellor Norman Lamont yesterday poured an extra £11 billion into public services to close the book on years of tight-money Thatcherism.*
>
> *He signalled massive increases for health, social security and jobs training and, in doing so, threw down the gauntlet to Labour on how it could possibly fund its own pre-election promises.*
>
> *After years of balancing the books, it could mean a Tory administration borrowing up to £19 billion next year to confront the effects of recession.*

(Again, these are extracts from longer pieces of text.)

The fog indexes are almost identical at 45. This is a middling figure, and is fine for news reporting. In each case, the writer has used considerable skill to simplify what could have been a foggy discussion of a foggy subject, economics.

This index should also be an upper limit for business reports, with both the average sentence length and the percentage of long words being in the low twenties.

(The identical fog indexes, by the way, might come as a surprise: the first piece is from *The Financial Times*, while the other is from *The Daily Mail*.)

Example 4

This last example is taken from a draft market research report.

> At the conclusion of the 1990 project, we identified a number of smaller, specialist suppliers with product, development and/or consultancy capabilities that may have proven of significant benefit to . . . in the development and realisation of this market opportunity.
>
> Through the bank interviews and the product evaluations, the development project will have the opportunity to compile a more comprehensive list of such smaller, specialist suppliers and their particular product, development and/or consultancy strengths.
>
> Profile evaluations may then be conducted on the selection of smaller, specialist suppliers with the most desirable market achievement, reputation, resource and capability, to determine the particular collaborative contribution and relationships that may be established with specific suppliers.
>
> Such collaborative partnerships may prove of considerable importance to the development and realisation of this market opportunity – as the 'product' solution will be seeking to satisfy a selection of specialist banking activity problems that will require a bespoke and distinct approach to the specific problems of each individual bank client – which will probably need to be consultancy led and to embrace the tailoring of developed product.

The total fog index is nearly 76. This is the highest we have ever recorded for a piece of real writing. (It was, of course, totally unacceptable, and the client never saw it in this form.) Almost all the nouns, verbs and adjectives are jargon of Latin origin. And not only that, the construction is over-complicated, with the sentences slithering down the page like writhing snakes.

What does it mean? Well may you ask!

COMPENSATING FOR JARGON

Technical terms and specialist jargon are, of course, sometimes unavoidable – the audience may expect them – so we have to compensate by simplifying the sentences. Again, this is taken from a real report:

> *Banks are universally worried about customer information systems, management information systems, marketing systems, and about delivery systems in general and, especially, support for direct sales functions at branch level. While we found that the requirements were not always clearly specified, there is no doubt that any new market entrant must be able to demonstrate that a new product will contribute to these objectives, even if it does not directly provide solutions.*

Here we have an average sentence length of 35, which is far too long, and a percentage of long words of 21.1, giving a total index of 56.1. Even if we leave in the jargon, we can still de-fog it by shortening the sentences and using simple terms wherever we can:

> *All banks are worried about customer information systems, management information systems, marketing systems, and about delivery systems in general. They are especially worried about supporting direct sales functions at branch level. Although such needs were not always clearly stated, new market entrants must be able to show how a new product will help, even if it does not provide a complete answer.*

The sentence length has come down from 35 to 20.7, because we have made the two sentences into three, and the percentage of long words has dropped from 21.1 to 14.5. Even within the constraints we set ourselves, we have still been able to cut the fog index from 56 to 35, a worthwhile reduction.

THE WICKED 'WHICH'

One easy way of shortening sentences is to keep an eye on the word 'which', and its personal friend 'who'. These are frequently used as substitutes for full stops, tying together sentences which ought to stand on their own.

Since we regard sales training as important, we are willing to assign two people to the team *which* will include our Sales Support Manager *who* is prepared to take on the administration and report to both of us periodically.

There are at least two viable sentences there, and possibly three:

Since we regard sales training as important, we are willing to assign two people to the team. One will be our Sales Support Manager. She is prepared to take on the administration and report to both of us periodically.

REDUNDANT WORDS

We can also reduce the average sentence length by simply cutting out unnecessary words. None of us would deliberately choose to make work for ourselves, yet we often use several words where one or two would do. What seems to happen is that we pace our writing to our brain, that is, we mark time while deciding what to put down next.

'At this moment in time . . .' What's wrong with 'currently', or even 'now'? Perhaps we do then pause while we think what should follow. So what? Nobody is watching and waiting . . .

Sometimes we pad out with words such as 'literally', 'certainly', 'definitely', 'basically', 'actually' or 'essentially'. They can add emphasis when used sparingly, but it's instructive to take the pruning shears to them and see exactly how little we lose:

CBT is literally student-paced. As we have seen, traditional classroom-based teaching methods essentially have difficulty in matching the basic speed of the course to varying levels of actual ability.

Supposing we just cut them:

CBT is student-paced. As we have seen, traditional classroom-based teaching methods have difficulty in matching the speed of the course to varying levels of ability.

In fact, the second version – without the emphasis – sounds more direct and positive, just because it's not carrying any passengers.

MAKING THE MESSAGE MEMORABLE

A little earlier, we were comparing two newspaper stories, one from *The Financial Times* and one from *The Daily Mail*. The fog indexes were almost the same, but one was a little more dramatic than the other. Why was this?

The Daily Mail writer tended to express the message in a very concrete and physical way. Rather than use abstracts, he or she found a way of making the statements very picturesque:

> *Chancellor Norman Lamont yesterday **poured** an extra £11 billion into public services to **close the book** on years of **tight-money** Thatcherism.*
> *He **signalled** massive increases for health, social security and jobs training and, in doing so, **threw down the gauntlet** to Labour on how it could possibly fund its own pre-election promises.*

Abstract ideas are very demanding for the audience. Not only do they usually entail the use of long words (so increasing the fog index), but they don't leave a graphic impression. It's easier to grasp the meaning if we can see a picture.

In other words:

Visualisation facilitates understanding and retention.

Or, to put it more physically:

Seeing it happen helps us understand it and remember it!

Thus we can make a more lasting impression if we can find physical and action-oriented metaphors to express the meaning:

A complete week's attendance at the Training Centre is having an unacceptably adverse effect on the sales force's productivity.

Clear, and understandable. But:

Pulling salesmen out of the field for a solid week is a luxury we cannot afford.

. . . is more memorable.

Such images can be very effective when we're dealing with dry subject matter, but the trick can become intrusive if we use it all the time. It's best, therefore, to reserve it for key sentences. That way, they'll stand out.

HANDLES

We can use the same technique to give our proposition an identity of its own. If we want our recommendation to be picked up and talked about by a variety of people, it helps if we can give it a 'handle'. If our audience can only draw upon vague and instantly forgettable phrases, there is less likelihood of our idea being passed around. A handle can also help differentiate our message if we suspect the audience may find it uncomfortably familiar.

The Fuddle CBT proposal fits both scenarios. The phrase 'the Sales proposal for a computer-based training programme' will not readily trip off everybody's lips in Accounts, IT, and Admin. And the shorter 'CBT' will simply be jargon to most of them. Also, as we are well aware, the reference to 'computer-based training' will be a touchy reminder to Training that they have already dismissed the whole idea.

We need a handle which is short and snappy, memorable, descriptive, and which sums up in a couple of words what's different about the proposal. Thinking about it systematically, the main attraction of CBT from Sales' point of view is the flexibility it offers. They don't have to send sales people away on a classroom course, and students can fit it into their normal selling day. At night, perhaps . . . How about the 'Moonlight Mentor'? Not quite right, since 'moonlighting' suggests other extra-curricular activities . . . What about 'Twilight Tutor'? It's far from perfect, but not bad. Perhaps the Sales Support Manager can discreetly offer it to her audience:

The salesmen are already enthusiastic about what they call the "Twilight Tutor"!

(N.B. A technique not to be used when writing objective reports!)

ACTIVE AND PASSIVE FORMS

We can also sharpen up the images we are conveying if we use active forms rather than passive forms.

- Active: 'We attended the course.'
- Passive: 'The course was attended.'

The passive form uses only the verb and the object, leaving a vacuum where the subject (or 'doer') should be. It's difficult for the audience to catch a mental image of what is happening.

In the Fuddle report, we may have drafted the following:

At least two orders were lost because visits to customers could not be accommodated at short notice.

Not only is there some question about exactly who the unfortunates were, but there is little impact.

Changing the passive form to the active, we can turn it into something more precise and unforgettable:

Two salesmen reported that they had lost orders because they were unable to visit their customers at short notice.

ROLE OF THE PASSIVE FORM

However, the passive form is there for us to use, and for very good reason. Since it focuses on the action and the object, we use it when the 'doer' is not relevant, or can be misleading. For example, a technical report might say:

The test run was successfully completed. However, when the engine was stripped down for examination, there was clear evidence of piston damage. It is likely that this would have soon resulted in catastrophic engine failure.

The passive form lends authority to the findings and to the opinion offered. If we had used the active form instead, the conclusions may lose objectivity:

The engineer completed the test run successfully. However, when he stripped the engine down for examination, he found the pistons were damaged. He thought this would have soon resulted in catastrophic engine failure.

The findings and opinion are now qualified by the audience's perception of the engineer's competence. The credibility could have been even weaker if we had named the engineer: a specific variable has now been included in the equation.

There could also be legal implications:

As soon as the matter had been brought to our attention, a full investigation was conducted. It was found that three other false expense claims had been submitted in the name of the individual during the last year.

Probably true. But if we had personalised it:

As soon as you brought the matter to my attention, I conducted a full investigation. I found that Steve had submitted three other false expense claims during the past year.

See you in court?

We can also use the passive form to avoid a sensitive issue. In the Fuddle report, we might write:

There are a number of possible solutions.

— The current courses could be revised;
— A new course could be bought from an outside provider;
— Sales training could be subcontracted altogether;
— Computer-based training could be considered again as an alternative to classroom-based teaching.

We have taken great care not to be specific about *who* might be exercising these options. By using the passive forms, we're avoiding any overt threats, or argument about responsibilities.

COMPATIBILITY

Much of what we have been saying may need adapting in some instances. So we have a rule to cater for this: it is compatibility that matters. The language we use should be compatible with language the audience expects.

Imagine the Marketing Director has been busy with his calculator and really going for the lowest possible fog index. He decides to discard this:

Our new marketing plan will therefore allow us to diversify into other new EC territories and generate a smoother revenue flow.

in favour of this:

Our new marketing plan will let us get into some more EC countries. It will also bring in the money more often.

Short and clear, but it will sound facetiously childish.

And in case we are suspected of bias against Latin words, we should mention that they will sometimes be preferable to Anglo-Saxon terms. When we're communicating in English with French, Spanish, and Italian speakers (not to mention Portuguese, Romanians, and speakers of Catalan, Provençal . . .), Latin-derived words may be clearer, since these languages are Latin-based. For such audiences, 'comprehension' might be easier than 'understanding'.

CARTOON-WRITING

In addition, over-enthusiasm for physical images can lead to excessive use of metaphors, and mixed metaphors.

American business writers and consultants seem to do this all the time. Companies don't get into financial trouble: they first 'bleed badly', then they 'go belly-up'! We call this 'cartoon writing', because it can read like a Tom and Jerry cartoon. Organisations become characters, and action is expressed in lurid terms.

The writers do this, presumably, to spice up what might otherwise be boring subject matter, but it can jerk European readers who are used to a more restrained treatment.

CREATING THE RIGHT IMPRESSION

The choice of language can have a powerful effect on the impression we create, especially if we combine it with what we know about affinities and angle.

Here's a letter written by the Personnel department to a job applicant:

The procedure in respect of applications for employment is that an introductory seminar is attended so that an appreciation of the company and its products can be acquired prior to the candidate progressing to the formal interview phase.

It uses a Neutral angle, and lots of passive forms. Although long-winded, it could be acceptable as an extract from an internal procedures manual.

However, when sent to an applicant, the angle becomes Author-angle (it's describing the company's policy without a thought for the reader's objectives), and no affinity is expressed.

Compare it with this:

We would like you to come to our introductory seminar to hear more about our company and the products we make. You can then decide whether you would like to come for an interview.

This is explaining exactly the same procedure, but this time the fog index is lower. The forms are active, making it easier to use Audience-angle, which in turn is expressing a Selling Affinity ('Let us help you decide whether to come and work with us . . .').

Which company would you prefer to work for?

USING HUMOUR

In the right circumstances, humour can be an effective weapon, but it can also be destructive.

On the plus side, it can:

- Relax the audience
- Defuse a sensitive situation;

- Reinforce tribal feeling;
- Make our message memorable;
- Allow us to express our own lovable personalities.

As an example, the Sales Support Manager might end the Fuddle report with the following:

If we can develop an effective CBT sales programme for our own use, this will not only increase our sales productivity, but also provide us with an opportunity to enhance our image. We would all prefer to see a photograph of our own Training Manager in CBT Monthly rather than some character from Banjax!

Remember that the poor Training Manager's courses have come in for a fair bit of bashing from Sales. This piece of mild humour might dispel some of the ill feeling. ('We all love him anyway . . .') And, with the 'us' and 'them' reference to Banjax, it will also strengthen the Fuddle tribal glue.

BUT . . .

The first caveat is our audience. If they have the sense of humour of a hangman, then it's better not to try to project ourselves as creatures of fun. Any attempt at humour would be a jerk. Even if we think we're really sure of our audience, it's still worthwhile thinking again. (We recall the manager who pinned a risqué memo to the notice board. Everybody thought it hilarious – everybody except for the chairman and the MD who arrived on a surprise visit the following day.)

Second, the audience may not always spot written humour. We are unable to give them any visual clues (relaxing, grinning, etc), so the words have to do the work. This makes it hard to get across certain types of humour.

Irony, for instance:

As his lawyers assured us, Robert Maxwell was a businessman of great integrity . . .

and sarcasm:

. . . and the reader would surely not expect us to suggest otherwise . . .

and understatement:

but the little matter of the missing pension funds may raise a few eyebrows.

These types of humour can easily be misunderstood if the background is not clear to the audience: the intended meaning is exactly the opposite of what the words literally say. (British authors especially should beware of understatement and self-deprecation. We're proud of our ability to laugh at ourselves but, as with so many of our national pastimes, the point of the game is not always clearly understood by a wider audience.)

On balance, attempts at such humour are not worth the risk.

And there will always be the little bit of entertainment we didn't intend at all:

We feel that the concept of CBT is now sufficiently promising to justify another investigation. The sales managers particularly like the idea of being able to do it at night in their own offices.

Even if we insist on being adventurous, we should remember never to make fun at the expense of:

- other strong tribal feelings (religion, politics)
- characteristics over which individuals have no control (nationality, age, size, appearance, IQ, sex, race, colour, disability . . .)

In these cases, not only will we offend the targets, but also others who feel obliged to take up cudgels on their behalf.

Summary

- Hook the audience!
- Use an informal structure for:
  - brief documents
  - informal documents (eg, sales letters)
- Use a formal structure for:
  - long, complex reports
  - meeting briefs (to facilitate verbal references)
  - operating manuals
- Use a covering letter if you need to:
  - reinforce the conclusions
  - send copies to different readers for different purposes
  - pass on something written by someone else
- Use an advance letter (or phone) when:
  - you are running late
  - conclusions or recommendations are unexpected
  - you want to make sure it receives special treatment
- Expand the outline smoothly and logically
- Encapsulate a discussion (facts, interpretations, conclusions) in one or more successive paragraphs
- When linking discussions, restate the conclusion instead of referring to another part of the text
- Begin a section with a heading or short positive key sentence which flags the subject covered
- Check for ambiguities
- Cut out redundant words and phrases
- Use shorter words of Anglo-Saxon origin, rather than long words of Latin or Greek origin
- Build them into short sentences, with as few conditional clauses as possible without losing the meaning
- Compensate for long technical words by shortening sentences instead

- Use physical terms and action to help the audience grasp an image
- Try to find a 'handle' for the proposition
- Use the active form to:
  - make the meaning clear
  - include the subject in the action (eg, in Author-angle, Audience-angle, Shared-angle messages)
- Use the passive form to:
  - focus on an event, effect or condition (eg, in Neutral-angle messages)
  - avoid implying a cause, intention or responsibility
- Use language appropriate to the audience
- Use language to create an impression compatible with your Aims, Affinity and Angle
- Use humour (if appropriate) to:
  - defuse a sensitive situation
  - reinforce tribal togetherness
- Never use irony, sarcasm or understatement when it might be misunderstood
- Never mock the afflicted or the fanatical.

12. Articulation – Numbers

The last chapter dealt with how to articulate the words of our argument. Now we shall be looking at numbers, and the use of tables and graphs in particular.

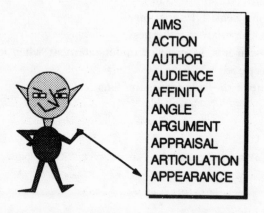

AIMS
ACTION
AUTHOR
AUDIENCE
AFFINITY
ANGLE
ARGUMENT
APPRAISAL
ARTICULATION
APPEARANCE

Much business information is concerned with figures, and many of our messages will be based on them, or will use them to make a point. Some audiences, like accountants and actuaries, love them, while others find them mysterious and threatening. We have to meet the needs of both. Just as the last chapter explained how to structure our document for the skip-reader, it makes sense to tailor our presentation of numbers to the kind of audience which is least comfortable with them. And at the same time, to keep in mind those who are doing their damnedest to prove we got our sums wrong.

Jim was once involved in looking at the introduction of flexible time working in the company. Several months' investigation suggested that the benefits would be considerable. Staggered attendance would relieve some of the problems arising from peak hour congestion in the city, and the idea appealed strongly to the work force.

He obtained proposals for the supply of machines to allow employees to clock in and out, and the price was affordable. Now all he had to do was to convince his conservative Managing Director, an accountant by training.

He asked for a meeting with the MD to discuss it, and to give the sales lady from the machine company a chance to present her credentials.

At first, the meeting went smoothly. The MD accepted the advantages, and Jim was able to deal with the few objections he raised. Then the sales lady made a brief presentation. She outlined some of the benefits that other companies had enjoyed as a result of flexible working, one of which was less absenteeism.

She explained that, with flexible working, employees felt able to take the odd hour off for personal reasons, and to make it up by coming in earlier or leaving later. With conventional nine-to-five working, they tended to 'go sick' for a whole day.

To underline the point, she put up a line graph which seemed to show a dramatic drop in absenteeism recorded by one of her customers.

The MD sat up and frowned. 'The graph carries no figures, but it appears to suggest a reduction of over eighty per cent. I find that implausible.'

'No,' she agreed. 'It was actually about ten per cent, I think.'

'You think?'

She reddened. 'I can't remember exactly, and I don't have the figures with me.'

'I see,' he replied testily. He stood and held out his hand towards her. 'I hope your machines are more painstaking with their accuracy Good morning.'

Jim had to find another machine supplier before the proposal was agreed.

Problems with numbers

- Not giving any numbers
- Giving too many numbers
- Implying unjustified precision
- Using meaningless numbers
- Putting too many numbers in the text
- Using the wrong types of graph
- Putting graphs and tables in the wrong place
- Misrepresenting numbers by doctoring graphs

NUMBERS OR NOT?

Do we need to give any numbers at all? The importance of numbers is obvious to some professions. Engineers, for instance, cannot do their jobs without accurate dimensions. Doctors seldom write a prescription with 'A little bottle of the biggish tablets, a few to be taken every now and then'. By comparison, financial numbers have had relatively restricted circulation in business until fairly recently.

In the past, some jobs were performed without much regard for money. The Chief Designer and his or her team got on with inventing the best product they could, and left the costs to the accountant tribe. Equally, the Marketing Director may have decided the company should set up a German subsidiary for strategic reasons, meaning that he felt it was important to the business but couldn't actually measure the benefit. Twentieth-century British history is full of initiatives which were acknowledged as good ideas at the time, but in the event were financial disasters – Concorde being a prime example.

As we know, things have changed. When times are good, there's enough fat for speculation, but when profits are thin, every proposition has to carry its own weight, financially-speaking. We now have to make all major business decisions with an eye on financial impact. 'What is this going to cost?' 'How much profit will this make?' These are common questions, and we now anticipate them as a matter of routine when we're building our message.

There are also some less obvious ones lurking beneath the surface, such as 'What is the impact on my budget? If I do this, what will I have to drop to make room?' 'Is this number consistent with the plan?' 'How reliable are these numbers anyway?' Such questions should have been predicted under SCORE, STALL and FAILURE in the Argument chapter, and of course, during the Appraisal in the context of assumptions. (If they weren't, it's still not too late to go back and check.) Ultimately, if our proposition has anything to do with money, we need figures to support our case.

GIVING TOO MANY NUMBERS

Numbers have a way of breeding. A few will quickly multiply, and before we know it, we have pages and pages of them. Why? Because computers (and spreadsheets in particular) provide exactly the right conditions for a population explosion.

For instance, our business plan can start with a projection of sales for Year One. Then, using assumptions about growth, we can soon set out numbers for all succeeding years. Since we know something about the cost make-up of the product, we can add another row in the model about manufacturing costs. We also have some assumptions about selling costs and indirect costs. That's another two. Now would you like to see it broken down by country? The model suddenly gives birth to fifteen others, and so it goes on.

It's easy to do, but does it really help?

UNWARRANTED PRECISION

For many audiences, numbers come with halos. If there is a number for it, it has to be right. Most people will demand we quantify terms such as 'approximately a lot', but are happy enough when we throw a few digits in their direction. The more digits there are, the more soothing the effect. 'Ten million' sounds a haphazard approximation, but few would argue with 10,251,634.

However, an important minority in our audience is wise to this ploy. They will treat any number with the greatest suspicion, and the more exact the number, the more they'll distrust it. Especially if we dress it up as market research:

The survey showed that 63.636 per cent of potential buyers thought our prices were too high.

Many of our audience would nod thoughtfully over this significant finding, but there will always be the character who eventually drags out of us that the sample was just eleven, of which seven said we were too pricey. We realise we should have said:

Based on a very small sample of around a dozen, it could be that over a half of possible buyers think our prices are too high.

And even then:

"Well they would, wouldn't they?"

No market research should ever be presented as accurate to more than a few percentage points, and only then if it deals with facts. Research figures which forecast intentions are often out by a very wide margin.

When we're presenting research findings, our audience will be trying to detect the guess or wish made up to look like a real number. In the above example, the respondents questioned in the survey had a vested interest in the conclusion: they wanted lower prices.

WHAT DO THE NUMBERS MEAN?

When we're thinking of using numbers to support a case, we ought to stop and ask whether they really do support what we're saying.

Scratching our heads over a set of figures, we tend to see what we want to see; conclusive proof of our point of view. However, numbers have an annoying habit of suddenly deserting us, or even changing sides.

The Fuddle Sales Support Manager is finalising her report on current training courses, and she may have just such a difficulty on her hands. She's staring at the set of sales figures provided by Accounts. She took their period sales figures for each sales person, and keyed them into a spreadsheet. She noted the dates each was trained, and then calculated the average period sales before and after training. The apparent end result was that sales had actually decreased after they had been trained! In other words, the sales courses are damaging sales. Great stuff! The figures come from impeccable sources, and Training will have to surrender. Or will they?

Suppose Training were showing her a set of numbers like this, except that they showed exactly the opposite? Would she accept their conclusion that sales were up because of training? Wouldn't she argue that any increase probably had more to do with hard work, dedication, recent price changes, the excellent support they receive, seasonal fluctuations, or a sudden increase in demand? Or simply normal variations in periodic figures? In fact, she could foresee a long and vigorous discussion about it.

So why should she expect Personnel to accept the opposite conclusion based upon her numbers? (She can see the arguments lining up. Recession. Lack of demand. Product problems. Holidays, or sickness? And something about silk purses and sow's ears . . .)

Forget it. The numbers are meaningless, or at best, inconclusive, so in the report somewhere she will mention that Sales did the exercise, but that they were unable to draw any reliable conclusions . . .

PRESENTING NUMBERS IN THE TEXT

If we have one or two numbers, we can normally include them in the text. Nobody would quote twenty numbers like this, but it's surprising how difficult it can be to read even a very few, especially when we are inviting the audience to compare them:

The survey also showed that the percentages of respondents who would consider buying our product was 31 per cent ("yes"), 48 per cent ("no") and 21 per cent ("don't know").

Having read the sentence, most people find they have to backtrack and check the numbers against each other to get the message. A jerk, in fact.

Even in this example, it might be better to set them out in a separate table:

The survey showed that the intentions of respondents who would consider buying our product were as follows:

Buy our product?	Per cent
YES	31
NO	48
DON'T KNOW	21

The numbers are easier to compare now that they are in a column, because that's the way we saw them when learning arithmetic at school.

Better still, we could express them in a graph. The numbers are represented pictorially, and we draw our conclusions in the accompanying text:

During the survey, over half the respondents said they would definitely buy or might buy our product.

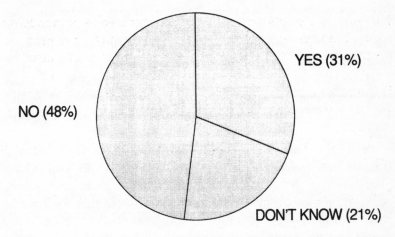

We can now grasp the (somewhat optimistic) conclusion much more easily. Our brains are much quicker at picking up analogue messages than digital ones. As a strategy for survival, estimating the distance between us and the tiger in terms of paces, and then using our calculating ability to work out relative speeds over the ground wouldn't be very practical. We have to decide *now* whether to run, and our eye can quickly determine the right course of action with more than enough accuracy.

In fact, the visual image is so dominant over words and numbers that we accept the picture, even though the numbers contradict what we see. To demonstrate this point during our workshops, we roughly follow the explanation we've given here. We then pause in case any of our students have anything to tell us. Only in one out of every three workshops will someone point out the error in the pie chart above. (The 'YES' and 'NO' labels have been transposed.) This is despite the fact that the attendees are managers with responsible positions, and well used to dealing with numbers every day of the week. The conclusion is that we should use graphs to make the conclusions as accessible as possible to our audience (but getting them right, naturally.)

TYPES OF GRAPH

Most spreadsheets offer a wide variety of graphing capabilities. We tend to use them simply because they're there, and it's easy to choose the wrong type. So here's a brief description of some of the more common types of graph found in business, and their uses.

Let's take another example from the world of Fuddle. You may recall from an earlier chapter that the MD has asked the Marketing Director to find out why sales of some products were not meeting targets.

Since then, the Marketing Director has been beavering away at the problem, and now he's found the answer: North Region have been selling the wrong product. They should have been concentrating on the new Eagle range, but instead they preferred to stick with the older and familiar Turkey product. (Perhaps they're waiting for the Albatross, the product which will solve all Fuddle's problems. This is two years away, and has been for five years . . .)

To support his conclusion, he has a set of numbers tabulated as follows:

Region	Product	1990	1991	1992	1993
NORTH	TURKEY	92,919	69,720	39,840	28,721
	CASHCOW	39,840	34,860	29,881	32,370
	EAGLE	4,980	5,478	7,470	8,466
	TOTAL	137,739	110,058	77,191	69,557
SOUTH	TURKEY	99,601	69,720	29,860	19,920
	CASHCOW	62,250	68,475	59,762	56,025
	EAGLE	9,960	29,877	74,699	124,500
	TOTAL	171,811	168,072	164,321	200,445
WEST	TURKEY	94,620	64,740	19,920	14,940
	CASHCOW	58,515	64,367	54,783	52,664
	EAGLE	7,470	24,898	64,740	109,560
	TOTAL	160,605	154,005	139,443	177,164
TOTAL		470,155	432,135	380,955	447,165
Company	Product	1990	1991	1992	1993
	TURKEY	287,140	204,180	89,620	63,581
	CASHCOW	160,605	167,702	144,426	141,059
	EAGLE	22,410	60,253	146,909	242,526

He came to his conclusion after studying the figures for some time, but now he has to present the evidence in such a way that the audience will quickly understand it.

SIMPLE BAR GRAPHS

This is the most common form of graph, and the most versatile. It's used to show voting intentions, for instance, when a quick glance shows which party is in the lead this time. In business, bar graphs are typically used to compare absolute numbers, often in a series of measurements over time. They are effective in giving an impression of year-on-year changes.

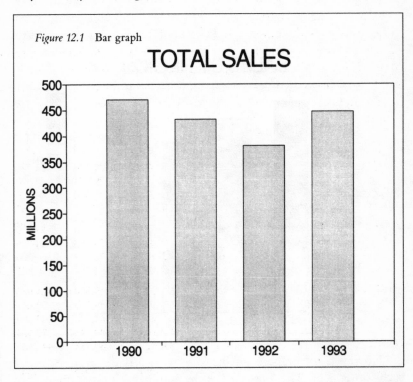

Figure 12.1   Bar graph

The Marketing Director might start his evidence by reminding his audience of the 'big picture'. He could show a summary of sales over the last four years, and he could do this with a simple bar graph as shown in Figure 12.1. The reasonable conclusion is that, after a couple of difficult years, things are looking brighter. 'Not bad, considering.'

STACKED BAR GRAPHS

Then he might show how the sales break down by region. He could use a stacked bar graph to show this. (Figure 12.2.)

Now his audience can see the reason for the concern. North Region has been on the slide for the last four years. The 1993 increase in total sales has been entirely due to South and West Regions.

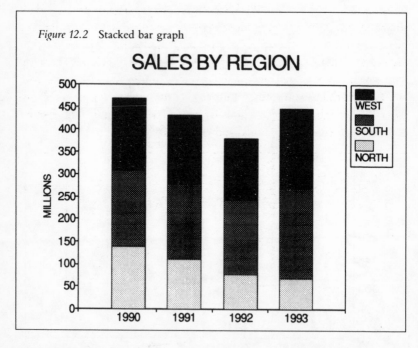

Figure 12.2   Stacked bar graph

However, the graph is unable to show clearly the progression of each component. The 'bottoms' of the South and West segments are at varying heights, making it hard to judge how much each of them increased or decreased over the four-year period. In addition, the numbers on the left (the Y-scale) are only usable for the total sales. To get at the sales figure for West Region in 1990, the audience has to do a quick bit of mental arithmetic, subtracting the number in line with the bottom of the segment from that at the top. To help the audience, we might insert the actual numbers alongside the various parts of the bars.

Alternatively, if our main focus is on the regional sales figures (as opposed to the total), we could do it another way.

LINE GRAPHS

Line graphs are similar to bar graphs, except that the values are represented by points linked by lines. Line graphs are good at showing progressions or trends. If more than one set of numbers is being used at the same time, a different type of line can be used to distinguish them from each other. We often see line charts showing the movement of share prices, exchange rates, interest rates, and so on.

The Fuddle Marketing Director might use Figure 12.3 to illustrate how the respective sales by region have been moving. Now the audience can easily spot the three trends.

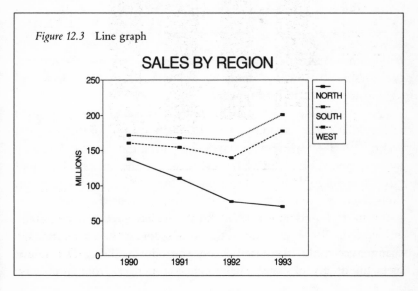

Figure 12.3   Line graph

There are, however, two potential problems with line graphs. Firstly, Figure 12.4 shows what can happen when the lines cross over.

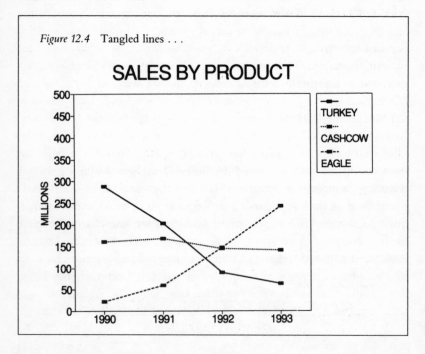

Figure 12.4 Tangled lines . . .

Although there are only three sets of numbers, each using a different type of line, the whole thing has become a bit of a tangle, and therefore difficult to read quickly.

Secondly, line charts can be easily misread. It's a mistake to assume that each year-point represents the beginning of the year, and that the line is showing what happened during the year. In fact, only the year-points on the line have any meaning: the lines serve only to direct our eye to the next measuring points. For instance, one might think from Figure 12.4 that the Turkey product ceased to be our best-seller in the middle of 1991. Such an interpretation is totally unfounded. We only know the totals for each year, and the changeover could have been at any time during 1992. This might seem blindingly obvious, but we have seen senior managers draw exactly this kind of unwarranted conclusion, leaving the more numerate among their audience shaking their heads in sad disbelief.

MULTIPLE BAR CHARTS

We can avoid these problems by using a variation of the bar chart instead. Figure 12.5 shows sales by product in North Region. Each product is represented by a vertical shaded bar. In fact, for the Marketing Director's purposes, this is a very telling chart. Sales of the outdated Turkey have been consistently falling, but North Region have failed to compensate with any significant increase in the sales of Eagle. We can more quickly see the relationship between them for any one year, and we are not tempted to say anything about what might or might not have happened in the middle of a year.

However, compared with an 'untangled' line graph, it is not quite so easy to follow the progression of individual elements, since we have to concentrate on one sort of shading at a time.

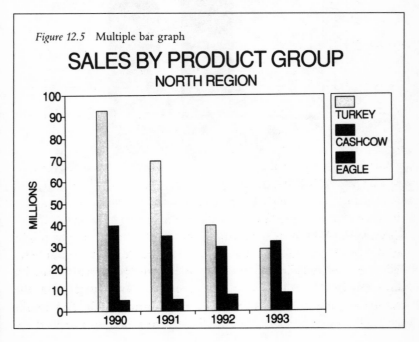

Figure 12.5 Multiple bar graph

SALES BY PRODUCT GROUP
NORTH REGION

3-D BAR CHARTS

In order to make such things clearer to see, some systems allow the use of 'three-dimensional' graphs. Figure 12.6 is an example, comparing the 1993 sales by product for each of the three regions. The added depth makes it easier for the eye to track the differences in sales for each product across the three regions. This is another important chart: while North have been persisting with the dying Turkey, South and West have been steaming ahead with the Eagle.

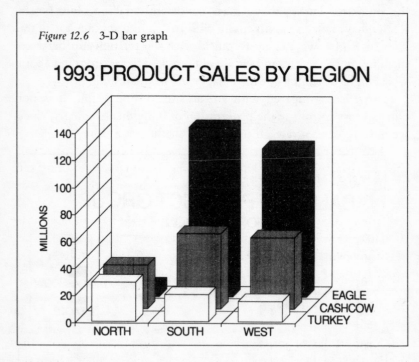

Figure 12.6 3-D bar graph

PIE GRAPHS

Pies are used only when the relationship of components is being discussed, not the whole. They offer a simple way of illustrating, for example, market shares, a breakdown of costs, or as in Figure 12.7, the results of some market research.

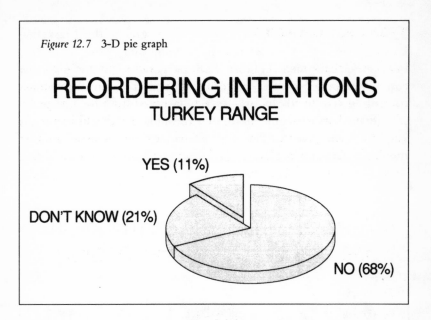

Figure 12.7   3-D pie graph

REORDERING INTENTIONS
TURKEY RANGE

YES (11%)

DON'T KNOW (21%)

NO (68%)

The survey commissioned by the Marketing Department showed that only 11 per cent of existing customers would buy the Turkey again, and is useful evidence to back up the contention that it's a dead Turkey.

However, we once saw a pie chart being used to show sales for the last five years, each year being a segment. This caused great confusion in the audience, and several minutes were wasted while the presenter had to explain repeatedly what he was showing.

X-Y GRAPHS

The last of the major types is the X-Y graph. This plots the relationship between one set of variables and another. A good everyday example would be vehicle speeds versus braking distances. X-Y graphs can also be used to show the effect on sales of increasing or reducing prices, or to produce 'scatter-grams', illustrating the deviation of a number of pieces of data from a norm. The positioning of the points can reveal patterns very much more quickly than a set of numbers in a table.

To give an example of a simple X-Y graph, the Marketing Director has in his possession a chart thoughtfully provided by the Personnel department. Figure 12.8 purports to show an exact correlation between sales performance and the number of days training given to the work-force, illustrated by the imaginary straight line which could be drawn through all the points on the graph. The message that Personnel are trying to get over is that more training means more sales.

Figure 12.8   X-Y graph

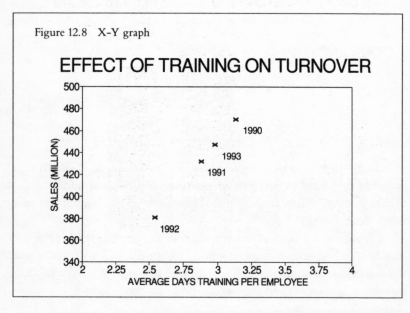

Although this type of graph is very useful in physics and engineering, it's less convincing when it is illustrating behaviour of people rather than things. There are typically many contributing causes for each effect, and such direct relationships are very rare. For this reason, the X-Y graph isn't often seen in day-to-day business management. In the case of the graph shown, the Marketing Director decides not to use it, for the same reasons that the Sales Support Manager discarded the sales figures from Accounts earlier. The sales performance over the last few years was down to a few factors besides the amount of training given.

ANNOTATING GRAPHS

Another facility we can use to make our graphs more understandable is to insert additional figures or comments in them. We can insert actual numbers in bar charts, or alongside points on a line graph. Like many other things, though, this can be overdone!

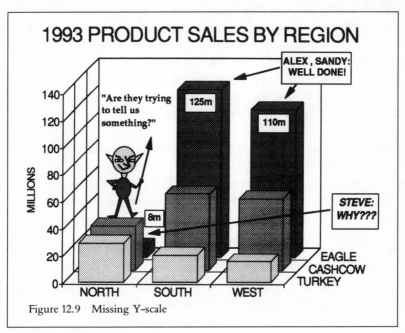

Figure 12.9   Missing Y–scale

INCLUDING TABLES AND GRAPHS

So where do we put them? The rules are:

* Graphs and tables should help the argument, not hinder it
* We should tell the audience *when* to look at them, and *where* to find them

In the past, we used to put all our tables and graphs in an appendix. This was for technical reasons – word-processors couldn't mix text and graphics – but we're sure our audience didn't thank us for it. Fortunately, most word-processors can now handle the two together, so we can juggle the words and pictures in such a way that the audience finds them natural and easy to use.

If graphs and tables are essential to the argument, we can insert them along with the text which refers to them, not forgetting to include a comment such as 'See Figure 5' when we want them to. (We have more to say on positioning tables and graphics in the next chapter.) If we are using graphs containing important numbers (and especially those provided by another party) we should really place the original figures in a table in an appendix.

DIRTY TRICKS WITH GRAPHS

Graphs are a powerful way of presenting evidence based upon numbers. At the same time, they are open to abuse. Graphs can be built in such a way that the audience is misled. The smart audience, though, is wise to these tricks, and is constantly on the lookout for them.

Three are illustrated on the following pages. (We explain them, not so they can be used, but only so they may be easily recognised and avoided.)

Missing Y-scale

The idea here is to omit the numbers from the vertical scale on the left, the Y-scale. The audience only sees different sizes of bars, but doesn't know what they actually represent. With Figure 12.10, for instance, the intention is to emphasise growth, as opposed to actual performance. The 1993 figure could be anything at all, 500 million, or 50. This one is a speciality of start-up companies.

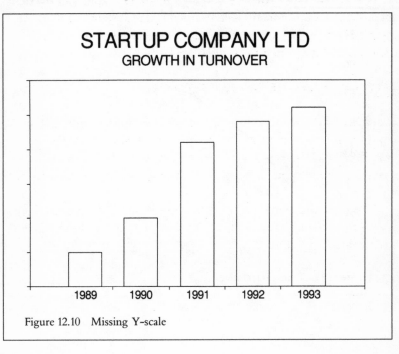

Figure 12.10   Missing Y-scale

Truncated Y-scale

This one starts the Y-scale at anything other than zero. It's used to magnify very small differences. In Figure 12.11, it looks as though the increase has been enormous, but in fact it is only a matter of five percentage points, and therefore probably insignificant.

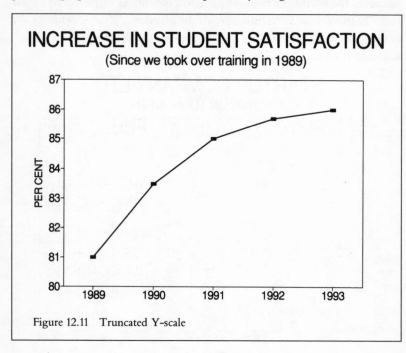

Figure 12.11   Truncated Y-scale

Logarithmic Y-scale

In this case, the Y-scale is not a linear progression, but is compressed as it moves upwards. The legitimate use for this is to focus attention on differences at the bottom of the graph, but it can also be used to minimise size differences, as Figure 12.12 shows. The eye reckons that 'THEM' is around three times larger than 'US', but in fact the true relationship is 100 to 1! This one is liked by small companies struggling against much larger competition.

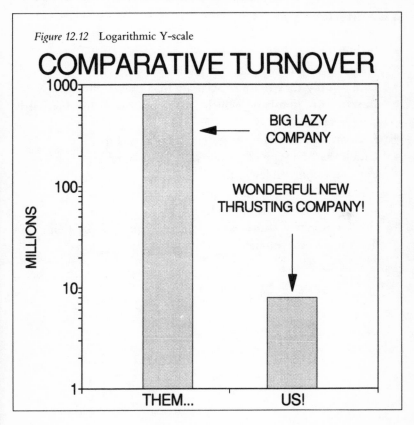

Figure 12.12 Logarithmic Y-scale

These three abuses are the most common. Though they can help an author present his case 'in the best possible light', using them in business even inadvertently will place our entire argument under suspicion. (The unfortunate sales lady at the beginning of the chapter would have been given the order if she hadn't used her numberless graph . . .)

In the last two chapters, we have covered how to present our words and numbers in such a way that our message will be clearly understood. The final part of our planning is concerned with the 'visual experience' our communication gives to our audience, and that's coming up next under Appearance.

SUMMARY

- Include numbers if the audience expects them
- Use only numbers which are relevant
- Don't imply they're more accurate than they really are
- Beware of numbers which may be open to alternative interpretation
- Put numbers in tables or graphs as far as possible
- Check that the type of graph is the most suitable
- Put graphs and tables in the right place
  - graphs and small tables along with the text
  - large tables in the appendix
- Beware of dirty tricks: know them when you see them, but don't use them yourself!

13. Appearance

This is the last 'A' in the 10A Technique, and it deals with the visual appearance of our document. The objective is to make the whole thing appealing at first glance, and to help make it legible.

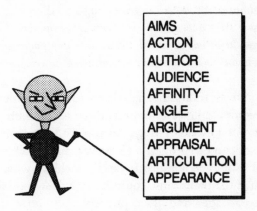

AIMS
ACTION
AUTHOR
AUDIENCE
AFFINITY
ANGLE
ARGUMENT
APPRAISAL
ARTICULATION
APPEARANCE

When discussing graphs in the previous chapter, we noted the fact that visual perception is extremely powerful. Similarly, the physical appearance of the communication could, if we get it wrong, destroy the message we have so carefully constructed – especially if we fail to meet the expectations of the audience:

Jim was settling into his job as computer manager with an insurance company. The time came to present the draft end-of-year accounts to the main board. He had an introduction neatly typed, and he appended to it several pages of printouts hot off the computer.

He triumphantly waltzed into the General Manager's office and presented the document personally. The General Manager, however, peered at it in horror over his pince-nez spectacles and then dropped it distastefully on to his mahogany desk. 'Mr Biggin,' he said, 'For the last hundred years, the Board of this company has been accustomed to receiving this report on vellum, and hand-written in Indian ink. I do not propose to discard this tradition simply in order to accommodate your new box of tricks. Please have the task completed in a fitting manner.'

When Jim returned to his own office, he was greeted by two grinning senior programmers. 'We knew that was going to happen,' they chortled.

'Good,' said Jim, 'so you won't be surprised when I tell you that I have volunteered you both to rewrite it.'

It took them a week to copy across all the numbers by hand, to read and check them, and to completely rewrite any pages with mistakes on them. The original computer run had taken just two hours.

Today, we have another factor to complicate matters. Before word-processors and laser printers, our communications were hacked out on typewriters by typists who had normally been trained to lay out a document properly. However, almost all of us now have on our desks (or even in our briefcases) machines which would have outperformed the mainframe computers of a few years back. Word-processing packages and laser printers now offer a bewildering choice of facilities, including scalable typefaces, automatic section numbering, page headers, and the inclusion of graphics. As a result, we can now do much more than ever before. But, as with spreadsheets, we often take advantage of these things simply because they're there.

Our guiding principle is to produce a document which will be easy to read. The end result may not be to professional design standards, but the techniques we offer should help our message, rather than hinder it. If our audience never comments on the appearance of our documents, we should take this as a compliment. The attractive presentation of a document is a bit like a good referee: we enjoy the match and never notice he's there. The appearance of a document is affected by:

- length
- covers and binding
- paper size and margins
- page numbering and page headers
- fonts and typefaces, method of highlighting, line lengths
- section numbering, paragraphing
- positioning of tables and graphs

There are two important warnings. First, some of what we shall be recommending impinges on the territory of the professional editor, designer or typesetter. We need to exercise restraint if we are producing a typescript for them to work their magic on. If our audience has asked for double-spaced Courier with 1.5" margins, then this is what they should get.

Second, many organisations have "house rules" which govern the appearance of documents, and these should be observed. To do otherwise is inviting trouble. The message received by the audience is that we're not willing to abide by tribal rules, as Jim discovered!

HOW LONG?

The length of the document has to match the requirements of the message to the expectation (and patience) of the audience. While it's not realistic to send a tome to anybody who has neither the time or inclination to wade through it, we shouldn't sell our message short simply because we happen to have read somewhere that all communications ought to fit on to a single page.

There isn't really a rule about this, other than 'no longer than it needs to be'. If the eventual length conflicts with what we judge to be the expectation and/or stamina of the audience, we produce a mini executive summary, perhaps in a covering letter.

COVERS AND BINDING

The use of covers and binding is dictated by the length of the document, its expected usage and life, and the impression we wish to create. There is no question that a solidly bound report looks as though it means serious business. A one-off memo needs no clothes, of course, but even a very short report to the board will normally be dressed for the occasion. In fact, many companies have house rules for this, if for nothing else.

PAPER SIZES

If we want the communication to be filed and retrieved, there is only one choice of paper size: A4 (210 × 297mm). Anything smaller, such as A5 (148 × 210mm), can get lost in the bottom of the filing drawer, and anything larger won't fit in it without bending! (If you have a moment, take a look in the bottom of one of your own filing cabinet drawers, and count the number of A5 brochures or letters you didn't know were there!)

MARGINS

Designers say we should leave plenty of white on a page, since too much print looks very daunting at first glance. About 2.5cm (1″) all round seems to work well, except that a 4cm (1.5″) left margin is normally needed to allow room for binding or punching.

PAGE NUMBERING AND HEADERS

We should always number pages if the document is longer than one sheet. The use of headers to identify the document can be useful if there is a danger that pages could become detached. Similarly, headers identifying the section can provide extra signposting. However, they can sometimes 'jerk' the reader if they are not kept distinct from the text. Leaving extra blank lines at the top of the page can help, but this tends to use space and make the communication longer. An alternative is to use a different typestyle.

FONTS AND TYPESTYLES

Until recently, the choice was limited. If we used a typewriter, then we were probably stuck with Courier. With the coming of laser printers, we now have access to a wide range of different fonts, usually available in different sizes measured in 'points' (a point being 1/72 of an inch). Just as we found with statistics and graphs in the preceding chapter, we are tempted to use them because they're there. When used judiciously, however, a suitable font can create the right impression.

Courier is the standard typewriter typeface, and is the one typeface which is available on all types of printer. It is a monospaced font, that is, the amount of space occupied by each character is the same. Originally, the only type of highlighting available was underlining, but matrix printers and lasers can also handle bold and italic.

Such printers can also cope with right justification, by expanding or compressing the spaces between words. (Printers which add whole spaces to achieve the same effect should be avoided, since it results in a "rivers of white" effect which can be distracting.)

Courier is universal, but now looks a little old-fashioned and – to some eyes – amateurish.

This is Times, sometimes known also as "Dutch". It is commonly seen in books, newspapers and magazines, but with the advent of laser printers, it is now widely used in business applications, and especially for reports. The classical typeface suggests an air of authority. It is a proportional font, with each character occupying as much space as it needs. <u>Underlining looks rather intrusive with this typeface</u>, so highlighting should be by using **bold or** *italic*, or ***even both***. The main advantage of Times is its compactness combined with legibility.

This is Helvetica. Variants such as "Swiss" or "Univers" look much the same. It has a more modern and informal appearance than Times, but otherwise has similar characteristics, including compactness.

However, it is not quite so readable in very small sizes, especially when a number of similar narrow characters appear together, as in the word "brillliant".

(Yes, there really were three "l"s in "brillliant"!)

Some printers support many more fonts than this, but these are the three most often used in business. Using some of the more arcane ones can result in a 'jerk'. In a newsletter we received recently, we were treated to a dose of Zapf Chancery Italic in the section headings. This particular font is not much good for anything except wedding invitations and diplomas. But it was in the printer's inventory, and the author probably thought: 'Why not?'

RECOMMENDATIONS – TYPEFACE

- Courier can be used as a general purpose, unobtrusive and generally accepted typeface, especially for short documents normally produced on a typewriter, such as letters or memos.
- Times or Helvetica gives a more professional appearance, especially where space is critical.
- Times and Helvetica may be combined. Times can be used for the main body of the text and Helvetica Bold for titles and section headings. Helvetica can also help distinguish text in graphs or tables from the main text.
- With the preceding exception, fonts should never be mixed for text within the same document.

(Yes, We know we broke the rules in this book. But this is to help distinguish the text from examples, and from the Goblin quotes!)

LINE LENGTH

One problem we never had with typewriters was line length. Laser printers allow us to use small point sizes and compact typefaces such as Times, and this can cause headaches. It can result in a line length which makes it almost impossible to read:

This is Times, sometimes known also as "Dutch". It is commonly seen in books, newspapers and magazines, but with the advent of laser printers, it is now widely used in business applications, and especially for reports. The classical typeface suggests an air of authority. It is a proportional font, with each character occupying as much space as it needs.

The line length here is about 85 characters, and is just about acceptable. If it were running across an A4 page, however, the length would be well over 100! The eye would have to track very accurately and would frequently go off the rails.

As a rule, lines should have a maximum of 60 to 70 characters, including spaces. We can achieve this either by increasing the page margins, by increasing point sizes, or both.

Newspapers get round this by having multiple columns, but we seldom see this device in business writing. Not only does it look odd out of context, but it's technically hard to do properly. The eye has to be steered carefully down one column, then to the top of the next, and around any graphics or tables. Even with professionally produced magazines, we sometimes lose our way, usually jumping to the top of the next column under a photo, instead of the top of the page.

SECTION NUMBERING

Numbering sections is very helpful with signposting. However, using several levels of numbering in a brief report looks too mechanical and unnecessarily formal. If we need to break up the points we want to make within a section, we can use bullet points instead.

Three levels of numbering are probably enough (eg 2.3.6) even for a long report. More than that, and it looks like a telephone number. Below three levels, we can again use un-numbered 'bulleting' to make the points separately. If we're convinced we need more than three levels, we probably need to reorganise our sections altogether: normally we find that one major section is causing the problem, and it would be better split into a number of smaller ones anyway.

The way we number sections is largely a matter of taste. Legal numbering (1.1.1 etc) is easier to use in discussions than a mix of numbers, Roman numerals, and upper and lower case letters. At a meeting or over the phone, it's much easier to say 'Can we now move to section 4.5.7?' than '4 e vii'! (Four, little 'e', Roman seven.)

In order to help with navigation, we can use margin release to put the numbers out to the left of the text:

2.2   Times is sometimes known also as "Dutch". It is commonly seen in books, newspapers and magazines, but with the advent of laser printers, it is now widely used in business applications, and especially for reports. The classical typeface suggests an air of authority. It is a proportional font, with each character occupying as much space as it needs.

Or we can use highlighted section headings:

2.2 Times

Times is sometimes known also as "Dutch". It is commonly seen in books, newspapers and magazines, but with the advent of laser printers, it is now widely used in business applications, and especially for reports. The classical typeface suggests an air of authority. It is a proportional font, with each character occupying as much space as it needs.

Or, even better, a combination of the two:

2.2 Times

Times is sometimes known also as "Dutch". It is commonly seen in books, newspapers and magazines, but with the advent of laser printers, it is now widely used in business applications, and especially for reports. The classical typeface suggests an air of authority. It is a proportional font, with each character occupying as much space as it needs.

PARAGRAPHING CONVENTIONS

Paragraphs may be separated either by an indent, or by extra spacing (eg a blank line), or (less commonly) both. A blank line is probably preferable for readability, but if space is really tight (as in a one page newsletter), using indents is a good second choice. The first paragraph in a section, however, should not be indented.

Some word-processors and printers now have the ability to vary the 'leading', the vertical distance between characters on different lines. Increasing the leading between paragraphs by a few points will give a useful little extra separation between them. In the next example, the leading between paragraphs has been increased by three points:

Helvetica (and its variants such as "Swiss" or "Univers") has a more modern and informal appearance than Times, but otherwise has similar characteristics, including compactness.

However, it is not quite so readable in very small sizes, especially when a number of similar narrow characters appear together, as in the word "brillliant".

(Yes, there really were three "l"s in "brillliant"!)

ORPHANS AND WIDOWS

'Orphans' and 'widows' need taking care of. If we start a section (or important paragraph) towards the bottom of a page, we might find we can only squeeze in the heading or the first line of text. This is an orphan. A widow is when the last line of a sentence spills over to the top of the next page. Not only do they look lost, but neither helps our skip-reading audience.

Most of the better word-processors can be made to avoid them. If not, we can simply get rid of an orphan by moving the section or paragraph to the next page. Dealing with a widow, on the other hand is not quite so easy. Moving the whole paragraph down might be a bit drastic, and if we interfere with the bottom margin to make room we might forget to change it back. If it looks too much of a 'jerk', the practical thing is to rework the text.

JUSTIFICATION

Right justification – to even up the ends of the lines of text – seems to work most naturally with proportional fonts such as Times or Helvetica. It's not nearly so successful with Courier, probably because it causes the space between words to vary, and the eye is used to fixed spacing with this font.

Right justification, however, may not always be appropriate with Times or Helvetica. It's fine when we indent paragraphs, but if we don't, the text tends to have a blockish look which some find unpleasant, as in this example:

> Right justification – to even up the ends of the lines of text – seems to work most naturally with some proportional fonts such as Times or Helvetica. It's not nearly so successful with Courier, probably because it causes the space between words to vary, and the eye is used to fixed spacing with this font.

> Right justification, however, may not always be appropriate with Times or Helvetica. It's fine when we indent paragraphs, but if we don't, the text tends to have a blockish look which some find unpleasant.

PLACEMENT OF TABLES AND GRAPHS

Any graphs or tables in an appendix should appear in the same order that they are referred to in the text, with clear descriptive numbering and titling. When in the text, tables and graphs should be placed as close as possible to the reference in the text. If we want the audience to read the text first, a good position for the graphic is to align it with the right margin, providing it leaves room for at least 20 characters per line for the text on the left. If, however, we want the audience to look at the graphic first, it could go on the left instead. This is where the eye naturally falls, and the reader will look at it before reading any following text. If the graph or table is too large to allow text alongside, it's best to break the text paragraph at the point where it's referred to, and slot it in there.

Occasionally, we need to insert a graphic towards the bottom of the page, but it won't fit. Referring the reader to a graph or table which is on the next page is a definite 'jerk', so it may be better (in business writing, we emphasise) to break the page early to avoid it. This might leave the bottom quarter of a page blank sometimes, but it's worth it. (Alternatively, we try reordering the argument a little to see if the problem can be sidestepped altogether.)

Though it's impossible to split graphics, tables do have a habit of wandering across page breaks. This is a 'jerk' if we're asking the audience to compare numbers in columns, so it's to be avoided if at all possible: again, it's better to break the page early.

One thing is a definite
and that's placing
of lines of text. The
time jumping over the
safely on the correct
To be fair, most word-
do this, but there are a
course, we are often
of trying it!

"no-no" with graphics,
them slap in the middle
audience has a very hard
graphic and landing
line on the other side.
processors don't let us
few which do, and of
seduced by the thought

BOXED GRAPHICS AND TABLES

One minor dilemma with graphs and tables is whether to put boxes around them. With one or two this can work well enough, but several boxed graphics can make the text look a little hemmed in. If the boxes are omitted, however, the titles of the graphics (or tables) can become confused with the main body of the text. To distinguish the two, we can use a different font or size for the graphic titles.

NUMBERING OF GRAPHS AND TABLES

Finally, before producing a final copy, it's always wise to go back and make sure the numbers and titles of all the tables or graphs are the same as those referred to in the text.

THE FINAL FUDDLE REPORT

What sort of visual experience would the final Fuddle report give the audience? On the next few pages, we set out a facsimile of what the covering letter and the report might look like. As you look at them, bear in mind that Fuddle doesn't have any house styles: it's everyone for themselves!

Fuddle

SALES DIVISION

Fuddle House
Meadow Park Estate
Reading, Berks RG44 0AA, U.K.

M. I. Laffin,
Director of Human Resources,
Fuddle Ltd.,
Brocklebank Way,
Basingstoke,
HANTS RG96, 7XX.

October 14, 1993.

Sales Training

Dear Malcolm,

I enclose two copies of a brief report on the subject of the current sales training.

From your memo of the 3rd, I know you already appreciate the need to improve the courses. You suggested that my department be involved in reviewing them, and this report is the result of our investigation.

You will see that we are making some very specific recommendations. Since the matter is one of high priority for the company, I propose we meet to discuss the findings as soon as possible.

I shall call you in a few days to fix up a time convenient to both of us.

The second copy is for the Training Manager. Although he was unable to take part in our meeting, I know he will be very interested in the outcome.

yours,

Ivan/

I. M. A. Winner
Director

Report on Fuddle Sales Training

Prepared by: I.M.A. Winner
Sales Director.

Date: October 14th, 1993.

Fuddle

Report on Fuddle Sales Training

1. Introduction

In this report, we assess the effectiveness of the company's current sales training, and make recommendations for improving it. The issue has become very important to the company because the sales force needs to operate at peak productivity in the current economic climate.

This report is the outcome of an investigation by Sales. We included an evaluation of the effect on sales performance and took into account the views of sales representatives who had been on the courses.

2. Conclusions

We recommend that Training, Sales and IT set up a joint task force to investigate computer-based training (CBT).

We understand that Training looked at CBT some time ago, and rejected it for what were probably good reasons at the time. However, it seems that the state of the CBT art has now progressed, and that the concept is now widely accepted. We therefore suggest we take another look at it.

If the findings are positive, we recommend we proceed to the piloting of a sales CBT programme.

3.   Background

As you know, the company has taken a number of urgent steps to improve our competitive position during the recession. We have recently introduced very keen pricing structures, and a number of improvements have been made to our current product range. We shall announce an important new product in a few weeks.

In order for us to reap maximum benefit from these moves, our sales force needs to work at high levels of competence. They should therefore have the best sales training that we can provide.

4.   Current sales training

Firstly, although we collected information relating to the performance of those salesmen who had attended the courses, a comparison of "before" and "after" figures proved inconclusive. The numbers show that sales performance was actually down following training, but we do not think this is significant.

Nor was there any noticeable difference between the performances of the salesman who had been trained, and those who had not. We feel that sales results over such a short period would have been affected by factors other than whether training had been given, or the quality of the training itself.

We attach more weight to the comments of the salesmen themselves.

Recent sales courses have not been well received by the sales representatives who have been on them. Their views seem genuine, and are unanimous.

They have expressed a number of criticisms:

4.1   The courses seem to vary in content. A comparison of the agendas for the courses in Weeks 12 and 15 shows major differences in both subject matter and scheduling. While there may be good reasons for this, it suggests that the courses are still in a state of development.

4.2   The courses are not based on selling our products. One course used examples of selling dog food, while the other was about selling what were termed "gizmos". This had an unsettling effect on the students. They found it very difficult to relate the sales techniques described to the products that we actually sell.

4.3   The recommended sales approaches were too aggressive. Some of the scripts were typically American, and quite unsuitable for use with our own prospects.

4.4   The courses were weak on handling objections. This is a very important subject, but only half a day was devoted to it. In the opinion of the attendees, this was not enough. As a result, many of them had problems with the role-playing exercises.

4.5   The courses did not cater for students with differing levels of ability. Some thought the pace too fast, while other found it hard to keep up.

4.6   The attendees found that being away at the Training Centre was very inconvenient. Two salesmen reported that they had lost orders because they were unable to visit their customers at short notice.

Our overall conclusion is that the current courses are not meeting the needs of the sales force. In particular, pulling salesmen out of the field for a solid week is a luxury we cannot afford.

5.   The alternatives

We recognise that there are a number of possible solutions.

- The current courses could be revised;
- A new course could be bought from an outside provider;
- Sales training could be subcontracted altogether;
- Computer-based training could be considered again as an alternative to classroom-based teaching.

At this stage, we cannot judge which would be the most cost-effective. **However, we feel that CBT should be looked at first, because it is the only solution which does not disrupt normal sales activity.**

6.   Computer-based training

To judge by comment in the press, CBT has a number of advantages. Some of these may have been overstated, but we also have the experience of one of our sales people who used it in her previous job.

6.1   CBT uses personal computers (PCs) to run the training program. Our own PCs might need more memory, but otherwise standard machines can be used. (A more detailed technical explanation is given in the attached article from CBT Monthly.)

6.2 Every student uses the same system and courseware. This avoids differences between courses, and variations resulting from a change of instructor. Sales training can therefore be standardised across the company.

6.3 CBT is student-paced. As we have seen, traditional classroom-based teaching methods have difficulty in matching the speed of the course to varying levels of ability. CBT allows each student to work at the speed most suitable for him or her.

6.4 CBT lets the student revise lessons as needed, and explore various options. There is not normally enough time on a classroom course to do this, so that individuals feel reluctant to ask the instructor to hold up the course and go over points again.

6.5 Salesmen can use it at virtually any time during office hours. Since CBT can run on the normal office PCs, they will not have to attend a training centre, and normal sales activity need not be interrupted. Salesmen can deal with urgent opportunities in the normal way.

6.6 It is clear that a number of organisations are now using it for a range of different types of teaching. (Actual cases are discussed in the CBT Monthly articles attached.) We also know that one of our main competitors, Banjax, is already using it specifically for sales training.

7. Recommendations

We recommend we set up a team to look again at CBT as a matter of priority, and to check out whether the advertised benefits are justified. We should start by contacting other users and asking for their experiences. We could also ask our consultants to research how far other people are happy with it in practice.

7.1 Scope of investigation

The investigation team should look at sales training only. This particular need is urgent, and we do not want the team distracted by having to consider what other types of instruction it could be suitable for. It might not be effective for our "Business Writing" course, for instance, and the team should not waste time worrying about such issues.

7.2 Timescales

Ideally, the task force should begin its investigation within one week, and deliver its report to us within a further eight weeks.

7.3   Investigation team

The team should consist of a joint "task force" of personnel from Training and Sales.

Although the company has not used this approach before, the task force is now very common, especially when projects require mixed skills. A useful by-product is that it breaks down departmental barriers and improves communications generally.

We are all having to work within tight budgets at the moment, but the commitment will be to provide heads for a limited period, rather than cash.

Since we regard sales training as important, we are willing to assign two people to the team. One will be our Sales Support Manager. She is prepared to take on the administration and report to both of us periodically.

From your own organisation, we think one person should be enough. As we understand it, the current sales training courses have been suspended, so you could choose the current sales instructor. Thus there should be little impact on your training schedules generally.

7.4   Location of team

We suggest the task force be based in the Training Centre, if possible. The Training representative will be a vital member of the team, and this will allow him to make easy reference to his files and to the existing courseware.

7.5   Involvement of IT department

We shall need help from the IT department on the technical issues. If you agree, we will approach to the IT Director to obtain his cooperation, and to arrange IT refresher courses for any team member who wants one.

If IT cannot for any reason be involved, we can use an outside CBT consultant.

8.   Pilot CBT programme

If the investigation produces positive results, we should then proceed to the development of a trial CBT sales course.

At this stage, it is not clear what might be involved, so until the task force has completed its investigation, we cannot discuss details. However, there are a few points we can make now.

8.1 The pilot will need funding. To secure this, we suggest that Personnel and Sales make a joint case to the MD to obtain funds from his contingency budget.

8.2 The specification for the system will be drawn up jointly by Training and very experienced sales managers. For the pilot, we would expect to be able to use a good proportion of the existing course material, and we will try to do this wherever we can.

8.3 It is important that the pilot concentrates on selling our actual products. If the pilot is successful, the courseware will be upgraded as new products are introduced.

8.4 At the end of the experiment, Training and Sales will together evaluate the results to decide whether to use it on a permanent basis.

The actual administration of the pilot will be under the management of Training, and the permanent adoption of a CBT sales programme would, of course, continue to be the responsibility of the Training department.

9. Summary

We feel that the concept of CBT is now sufficiently promising to justify another investigation. The sales managers particularly like the idea of being able to have access to training in their own offices. (They are already enthusiastic about what they call the "Twilight Tutor"!)
If we can develop an effective CBT sales programme for our own use, this will not only increase our sales productivity, but also provide us with an opportunity to enhance our image. We would all prefer to see a photograph of our own Training Manager in CBT Monthly rather than some character from Banjax!

Did it work?

Of course. Didn't you see the article in last month's 2CBT Monthly? Admittedly the photo was of the Sales Support Manager rather than the Training Manager, but she now knows how to **'manage her message'**!

That rounds off our explanation of the 10A Technique. In the final chapter – Application – we'll be offering a few tips on how to use it in practice, along with a few examples of difficult and important situations, the completed 10A Forms in each case, and the letters which were produced as a result.

SUMMARY

- Obey specific document layout instructions from the audience
- Observe any house rules
- Document length should match argument
    - If it exceeds the audience's expectation or possible patience, produce summary document, or covering letter
- Use binding and covers to suit length, expected life, desired image
- Leave adequate margins (1″ minimum all round on A4)
- Use page numbering for documents over one page in length
- Choose the font (where available) to create the right image
- Don't mix typefaces in same document (other than using Helvetica for headings and Times for text)
- Only use underline for highlighting Courier
- Use a maximum line length of 60 to 70 characters
- Don't overdo section numbering in short documents
- In long ones, three levels is enough
    - use bulleting below third level
- Section numbering is best in legal format (1.2.3 etc)
- Separate the paragraphs with a blank line or indent
- Look after widows and orphans
- Don't right-justify un-indented paragraphs
- Place tables and graphs in the same order as they are referred to in the text, with clear descriptive numbering and titling

- When in the text, tables and graphs should be placed as close as possible to the reference
- Avoid splitting a table across a page break
- Never place a table or graphic in the middle of lines of text
- Distinguish text in table or graph titles from the main text
- Make sure numbers and titles of tables or graphs are the same as those referred to in the text
- Never send anything until you have read it first!

From: Sales Support Manager
To: Personnel Director

Just a note to thank you for your help with the preparation of the report. Without your suggestions, we could have finished it within three days.

There's a little word missing. The word is 'not', and it should have come after 'could.' This time, the Goblin isn't saying anything . . .

14. Application

Having invested your time in reading about the 10A Technique, you may be wondering what it's like to use in practice. Although a very powerful tool for managing messages, it does, like everything else worthwhile, take a bit of getting used to. At first, you may find the process a little forced, but we promise you that it quickly becomes much easier after you have used it a few times.

It's not that the 10A Technique will enable you to do things you couldn't otherwise do. It's the discipline of going through the ten As and using them as a checklist which makes all the difference.

After a short while, you will discover that:

CHECKLIST

- Thinking about Aims and Action soon becomes automatic, although you'll frequently change your mind during the planning process. It helps keep focus on what you're trying to achieve, which is no bad thing.
- Author and Audience are usually obvious, but will sometimes need thought, particularly when you're wondering about the competence or motivation of the latter.
- The Affinity will cause most head-scratching. It's the nub of the whole motivation issue, and it will occasionally make you go back and change something about Aims in order for the proposition to become workable. The requests ('let's work together to . .' and so on), will give you a flying start with the argument. And the Angle, which is tied directly to the Affinity, soon gets the mind in the right viewing position. After a while, you'll find you won't need the conscious use of 'we' or 'you' to do this.

- Probably the most valuable and versatile part of the whole technique, however, is the SCORE, STALL and FAILURE methodology under Argument. Although at first you might have a problem remembering what the acronyms stand for (hence the SSF Form in the Appendix), you'll find yourself applying it in the most surprising circumstances. When you come across a proposition which succeeded or failed spectacularly, you'll always be able to see why.

- Articulation will be the hardest to apply methodically. It takes some time to adjust one's style of writing to suit particular situations, but it comes with practice. Even a small improvement can make a huge difference to readability, even if it's only cutting down your Fog Index!

- Appearance – though the most technical – will actually be the easiest if you have a word-processor. Invest a little effort in making up some style-sheets, and then you can 'fire and forget'!

FINAL TIPS

- When reading a newspaper, magazine, or a piece of junk mail, stand back from it and look at it as a piece of writing. Try to work out what's good or bad about it, and how the author could have done it better.

- If you find the 10A Technique useful, persuade your subordinates to use it as well.

- Don't bother to use the 10A Technique for messages in Valentine cards etc – we know all too well that the whole thing can become an obsession if you're not careful!

Finally, our policy is one of continuous improvement. If you have any constructive comments or suggestions, please drop us a line, care of our publisher.

AND REALLY FINALLY . . .

We'll finish the book with a few examples of how to use the 10A

Technique in some awkward situations. You might find them useful if you're in a similar fix! In each case, we outline the problem, then give a 'wrong' solution, then apply the 10A Technique (including SCORE, STALL and FAILURE), and finally offer a suggested solution. (We'll be concentrating on content, rather than appearance and, in the interests of brevity, the SCORE, STALL and FAILURE analyses will be slotted into the 10A Forms rather than appearing on a separate sheet.)

There are, of course, no perfect answers to any of the situations. When you see how we have filled in the 10A Forms, you may well come up with different and better versions. As we said in the Introduction, the 10A Technique will encourage you to use your imagination and express your personality when you come to *Manage The Message* for yourself.

CASE 1

You are a departmental manager. For two years, you waited in vain for the IT department to design and install a computer system for you and your people. Finally, you lost patience and ordered a system from an outside software house. Your organisation's IT manager had pointed out that the supplier is not on the approved list, and he had strongly advised you not to use them.

The system has now been installed for six months. Not only does the hardware keep breaking down, but the software is full of bugs! The software house has been trying very hard to put matters right, but their rep now tells you the system is out of warranty in accordance with the terms of the contract you signed. From here on, you will have to pay for support.

The IT manager is unsympathetic. He doesn't have the resources to help. You took the risk against his advice, and now you must sort your own mess out.

Your only solution is a letter to the software house.

From: Departmental manager
To: Software house rep

I was shocked to learn that you intend to keep us to the letter of the contract, and withdraw support unless we pay through the nose. We are certainly not going to be held to ransom like this. You know very well that the system you installed is a load of rubbish, and that your people are incapable of sorting it out. I am writing to tell you that if, by the end of the month, the system is not performing perfectly in all respects, I am going to take the following action.

1. I am going to write to all the magazines and tell them what cowboys you are.

2. I shall get one of your competitors to clear up the mess and send you the bill.

3. I shall start legal action against you for selling goods of unmerchantable quality.

I hope you go bust.

Analysis

Everything is wrong, the letter is simply threatening. The rep might be frightened into doing something positive, but it's doubtful. Because legal action is being threatened, he'll refer it to his director. Along with several reasons why it was all your fault, rather than theirs.

His director will read it, and decide that you're probably speaking for yourself and not for your company, and that you're trying to cover up your own mistakes. The threats themselves don't sound very well considered: you're just lashing out. He'll probably decide to treat you to a slap-up lunch, and talk you into buying an upgraded system, or signing a hefty support contract, or both. Apart from the possible lunch, you lose either way.

10A Form for: Software house problem.

1. **Aims** (operational objective)
   get the system fixed.
2. **Action** (desired effect of the communication)
   change h/w, s/w, support people? continue free support.
3. **Author** (sender of the communication)
   you. buyer of system. tribe = company. aim = good systems.
4. **Audience** (recipients of the communication)
   md of software house. tribe = supplier. aim = more business.
5. **Affinity** (relationship between author and audience)
   selling: "Let me help you sell more to my company."
6. **Angle** (point of view to be adopted)
   audience.
7. **Argument** (supporting reasoning)

Synergistic: you want easy life too. you might get more sales.
Compatible: normal practice by competitors.
Opportune: urgent. IT reviewing approved supplier list.
Rewarding: become approved supplier, more sales to us.
Easy: little cost to you (manufacturers' warranty?) people, not cash.
Suspicion: not trying to hide anything.
Theology: normal practice.
Aberration: (ditto)
Linkage:
Low priority: urgent now.
Funding:
Abasement: normal practice.
Investment: why throw away relationship and effort already spent?
Lock-in: not create precedent. approved list rules set out duties.
Uncertainty:
Risk: avoid greater risks.
Expertise: you have skills and resources.

   background.
       company has approved list, reviewed frequently.
       many orders placed every year, but you're not on it.
   current system has more than fair share of problems.
       needs sorting quickly.
   suggestion:
       obviously need to change h/w, s/w, people
           normal practice by your competitors.
       some products under manufacturers' warranty?
       discuss qualifications for approved list.

8. **Appraisal** (checkpoint)
   OK.
9. **Articulation** (how the communication is expressed)
   informal, but firm.
10. **Appearance** (physical appearance of the communication)
    short letter with company letterhead.

Fuddle

Fuddle House
Meadow Park Estate
Reading, Berks RG44 0AA, U.K.

R. Pitcher, Esq.,
Managing Director,
ACME Systems Ltd.,
239 Peach Street,
Wokingham, Berks.

October 25th, 1993.

Dear Sir,

My company places a great deal of business every year with organisations like yours.

Although your company is not on our approved supplier list, my department purchased a system from you in the expectation that the service you would provide would meet the normal standards. We were very impressed with your original proposals, and we looked forward to a long and mutually beneficial relationship between our companies.

However, we have been experiencing more than our fair share of difficulties with the new system. This must be as much a matter of concern to you as it is to us. Your support people have invested a great deal of time and effort over the last six months, but problems continue to occur.

You will doubtless agree that a solution has to be found urgently.

Normally, our suppliers react very quickly to such situations, and it is standard practice for them to replace faulty hardware and software under the manufacturers' warranty and at no charge to us. In addition, they usually extend the initial contractual support period, and assign senior support staff to iron out any remaining problems. By doing this, they continue to enjoy our trust and confidence.

I am sure you would like to enjoy a similar relationship.

Can I suggest we meet to discuss which of these steps would be appropriate under the circumstances? At the same time, I could let you have a copy of the normal terms and conditions in force with our approved suppliers. Now would be a good time for you to consider making a formal application to be added to the list, since I suspect my company will enforce the rules more strictly in future.

Naturally, we will be pleased to support your application once our system is running satisfactorily.

Yours faithfully,

J. Mugg,
Manager, Printing Services.

CASE 2

Your company has offices in the city, and you manage a team of highly-qualified specialist staff. They would not find it difficult to get alternative jobs with your competitors.

Following a recent merger, your company has decided to relocate a number of departments – including yours – to a new 'green field' site in Grimford, a town not unlike Milton Keynes. A generous relocation package is on offer. The company expects you to use your persuasive skills to encourage your staff to relocate with you.

From: Manager
To: All staff

By now, you will all have heard that this department will be relocating to Grimford. This has come as a shock to all of us, but I suppose we were expecting something along those lines after the takeover, but like you I was rather hoping they would let us stay put. To be fair, I have now received details of the relocation package, and on the face of it, it seems a good deal. Sam will be circulating your copies in due course. She also has a map of the area. I would warn you though, if you want to take up the offer, you have to confirm it in writing by the end of the month. If you do not want to go, the company is saying they will do their best to find other jobs for you, but I think redundancy is obviously on the cards. I do not know what the terms of that will be yet.

Analysis

Just one of the lads – natural, honest, open. He writes as he speaks, that is, without thinking about it too much. The main problem, however, is that his people have to do all the work. What is the company trying to achieve? What does the package include? Are there any other benefits in relocating? How do they decide? If any of his staff do agree to relocate, it will not be as a result of anything the writer said! On the other hand, an attempt to sell the idea would be equally wrong:

You will all be pleased to hear that the company has decided to relocate us to Grimford.

As you know, Grimford is a very attractive new town set in the middle of the beautiful countryside. It has new schools, plenty of leisure facilities, and an impressive shopping complex. Traffic problems are unknown!

Moreover, the relocation package on offer is very generous. None of you will lose out financially.

This team has worked together extremely well for the past few years, and I know you will all want to stay together as a winning side!

Please confirm that you will take advantage of this offer.

Even if some of the more gullible take him at his word, there will be trouble sooner or later when they find out that neither Grimford or the financial arrangements are what the writer cracked them up to be. The right approach is to make it as easy as possible for the staff to make the decision which is best for them. This needs a constructive Action.

10A Form for: Announcement of relocation to Grimford

1. **Aims** (operational objective)
    inform staff, encourage to relocate.
2. **Action** (desired effect of the communication)
    come on day-visit to Grimford.
3. **Author** (sender of the communication)
    manager of team. tribe = team/company/family man. aims = keep team together/happy team/happy partner.
4. **Audience** (recipients of the communication)
    team. tribe = team/company/family heads. aims = make right decision/happy partners.
5. **Affinity** (relationship between author and audience)
    teamwork. "Let's take a look together and decide."
6. **Angle** (point of view to be adopted)
    shared.
7. **Argument** (supporting reasoning)

Synergistic: discuss package, look at town, partner involved.
Compatible: we work as a team, like always.
Opportune: need to make a decision soon.
Rewarding: see it, discuss it, make nice day out.
Easy: we make arrangements and pay.
Suspicion: not trying to sell you.
Theology:
Aberration: lots of other companies do the same.
Linkage: no obligation.
Low priority: top priority.
Funding: company pays.
Abasement:
Investment:
Lock-in: no obligation.
Uncertainty:
Risk: none.
Expertise: none needed.

    announce relocation.
        reasons.
            claimed advantages.
            others moving there.
        relocation package.
            apparently generous, but needs study.
    suggestion.
        team and partners on day out.
          see for themselves.
        overnight hotel, plus explanation of package, discussion.

8. **Appraisal** (checkpoint)
    OK.
9. **Articulation** (how the communication is expressed)
    informal.
10. **Appearance** (physical appearance of the communication)
    memo.

MEMO

To: All members of staff
From: John Brown, Manager.

October 25th, 1993

Relocation to Grimford

Following the recent merger, the company has decided to relocate certain departments – including ours – to new offices.

After a great deal of research, Grimford was selected as the best all-round solution. A number of other major companies have already moved there, and the town seems to offer a great deal in terms of facilities for education, leisure and shopping.

The company has also announced a financial relocation package which is intended to defray any costs involved. It is rather complicated, but it seems generous. (Your copies are on the way.)

This team has worked extremely well for the past few years, and the company would like us all to stay together as a winning side. However, I know that you will all want to weigh up what is involved and make the decision which is right for you and your families.

So I'm taking you all on an outing, courtesy of the company! I have made arrangements for us all – and our partners – to visit Grimford next Friday and take a look at it. We will stay overnight at a good hotel, and return the following morning.

The coach will leave at nine. We'll have a conducted tour of the town (with lunch of course). In the evening, we will have a meeting, and I will do my best to explain the relocation package. A local estate agent will be on hand to talk about housing. Then we can all discuss it over dinner.

If the timing is not convenient for your partners, I will pay for you and your partner to go another day on your own. But I won't be able to fix a personal conducted tour!

Please confirm to Sam that you can come.

Yours,

John.

CASE 3

In a huge blaze of national publicity, two of your directors have been found guilty of fraud and sent to prison. The Managing Director has decided to write to customers to try to restore confidence. As customer relations manager, you have been asked to draft a letter for him.

As you will have seen in the national press, two of our directors have unfortunately been convicted of fraud, as a result of which a small number of our very largest clients suffered considerable losses. Your company was not involved in any of the illegal transactions.

The two individuals concerned have now been dismissed. Our internal procedures have been reviewed, and there will be no repetition of this incident.

We trust we will continue to enjoy your valued custom.

Analysis

The audience is left wondering whether the MD is less worried about the fraud than the fact that the fraudsters were caught! As for the dismissals: what choice did the MD have now they're in jail? If the procedures needed tightening that much, what else may have been going on?

Apart from that, the letter makes no attempt to express any kind of affinity, other than the hopeful little bit of pleading at the end. There is no real Action, other than 'audience read the letter' perhaps. What could we have as an Action which will contribute to the Aims?

10A Form for: Fraud problem.

1. **Aims (operational objective)**
   continue trading.

2. **Action (desired effect of the communication)**
   come to our "open morning" meeting.

3. **Author** (sender of the communication)
   md. tribe = company/supplier. aims = restore confidence/continue trading.

4. **Audience** (recipients of the communication)
   MDs. tribe = customers. aims = deal with safe suppliers.

5. **Affinity** (relationship between author and audience)
   selling. "Let me help you relax."

6. **Angle** (point of view to be adopted)
   audience.

7. **Argument** (supporting reasoning)

Synergistic: meet new directors, hear about new products.
Compatible:
Opportune: need reassurance now.
Rewarding: you will be able to relax.
Easy: just come.
Suspicion: !!! we'll tell you all about it.
Theology: none.
Aberration: none.
Linkage: none. no obligation to trade with us.
Low priority:
Funding: none.
Abasement: none.
Investment: none.
Lock-in: no obligation.
Uncertainty: we'll be specific.
Risk: none.
Expertise: none. but bring your controller if you want.

   background.
       only two involved.
       we discovered fraud.
   measures taken.
       compensation.
       tightened procedures.
   invitation.
       come to "open morning" meeting.
       we'll explain situation.
         answer questions
       introduce new directors.
       talk about future plans.

8. **Appraisal** (checkpoint)
   OK.

9. **Articulation** (how the communication is expressed)
   Short letter, friendly, open.

10. **Appearance** (physical appearance of the communication)
    standard company letter.

BANJAX

Banjax House
Meadow park Estate
Reading, Berks RG44 0AA, U.K.

From the office of the Managing Director

J. Smithers,
Managing Director,
ACME Manufacturing Ltd.,
Fountain Way,
Slough, Berks.

October 25th, 1993

Dear Mr Smithers,

You may be aware from the press that two of our directors have just been convicted of fraud. I am writing personally to you – one of our most important customers – to explain the situation, and to reassure both you and your directors that you need have no reservations about continuing to do business with us.

First, the facts.

It was we who discovered the fraud and brought the matter to the attention of the authorities. Only two individuals were implicated.

Although the amounts involved were large, only a very few of our customers were affected. They have been fully compensated for any losses.

Our procedures were already meticulous, but we have now tightened them even further. We are confident that there will be no repetition.

On the other hand, we are conscious that our image has suffered badly in this affair. I know you – and all our other customers – have always relied on the quality of our products and the integrity of our organisation, so we understand the worries you must have.

We are therefore holding a special "Open Morning" for selected customers, and I would like you and your directors to come so we can put your minds at rest.

You can hear in more detail exactly what happened, and what we have done to ensure it never happens again. I shall be very pleased to answer any questions you may have, on this or any other subject.

I will introduce our new directors to you, and outline some future plans which I know you will find of interest.

My personal assistant will call you with the details and to confirm that you can attend.

We all very much look forward to seeing you.

I might even tell you how we caught the blighters!

Yours sincerely,

Gerald Blush,
Managing Director.

CASE 4

This is a very common one, and one which few people seem to get right in real life.

> *You work for a supermarket chain. The company is applying for planning permission to build a new superstore on a rural site in a small but affluent village called Upper Nimby. Upper Nimby lies between the two towns of Ruffshod and Blowham.*
>
> *The company has asked you to insert a small piece in the planning application to the Ruffshod & Blowham District Council – the planning authority – in order to sell the idea.*

The new Cheapway superstore will bring many benefits to the community.

Our research shows that there is a need for a new superstore to serve Ruffshod and Blowham. At the moment, the nearest such amenity is in Grimford, a distance of fifteen miles.

With 36 checkout lanes, the new store will be the largest in the area. The store will be open from 8am to 8pm every day of the week, and will carry the full range of Cheapway lines at our usual low prices. It will have an off-licence and a cut-price petrol filling station. There will be free car parking space for 500 cars.

The store will create a number of new jobs, both full-time and part-time. Cheapway is an equal opportunities employer, and the new positions will be open to all regardless of age, colour or sex.

Analysis

The application will, of course, be rejected unanimously because of complications with our Audience.

The planning application is addressed to the Ruffshod & Blowham D.C. planning officers, and they will make recommendations to a planning committee which makes the decision. The committee is made up of elected Ruffshod & Blowham D.C. councillors, one of whom may have Upper Nimby in his/her constituency. Upper Nimby also has an elected Parish Council. It will expect to be consulted by the district council, but doesn't get to vote.

So who is the Audience? In many instances, and until recently, it wouldn't have mattered. Unless a cabinet minister happened to live in Upper Nimby, the application would have been quietly approved by Ruffshod & Blowham D.C. on the basis of the shopping needs of the whole area and the employment opportunities. Upper Nimby Parish Council would seethe in vain. Most of the Upper Nimby residents would find out about it the day the bulldozers moved in . . .

But not any more. Many villages like Upper Nimby have discovered "resident power", and have shown themselves quite capable of banding together to fight off such applications, especially if they can raise the cash for legal and expert representation. The flag they wave is 'conserving the environment'.

Planning authorities are now well aware of this, and politicians being what they are, Upper Nimby will be very much in their thoughts. The application will fail because Ruffshod & Blowham officers and councillors will be nervous about the reaction from the local residents. This will show up under STALL and FAILURE:

Suspicion:
Theology: environmental issues will be raised.
Aberration: we don't give permission to build these things in a peaceful village like Upper Nimby any more.
Linkage: Upper Nimby residents will have to agree.
Low priority: we don't need this problem now.
Funding:
Abasement: we will look stupid and uncaring if Upper Nimby nobbles the media.
Investment: some of us have friends and employers living there.
Lock-in: we won't be able to change our minds later.
Uncertainty: some of us could lose our jobs over this.
Risk: the whole situation is fraught!
Expertise: we won't be able to cope with the articulate doctors, vets, lawyers, pensions advisers etc who live there.

So the tribe that has to be won over is the one living in Upper Nimby itself.

However, a quick application of SCORE, STALL and FAILURE shows that this too is impossible:

Synergistic:	not at all.
Compatible:	not at all.
Opportune:	not at all.
Rewarding:	not at all. we shop at village store. anyway, it's only ten minutes by BMW to Grimford.
Easy:	very difficult for all of us.
Suspicion:	what will they do next?
Theology:	it will ruin the environment.
Aberration:	you don't build these things in a peaceful village like ours.
Linkage:	it will be a DIY superstore later.
Low priority:	we need a new village hall and cricket pavilion first.
Funding:	we can't afford to sell up and move out at the moment.
Abasement:	even lower property values. noisy traffic. unruly visitors. litter. ruined sundays. environment. public health and safety. etc. etc. etc.
Investment:	property.
Lock-in:	we'll be stuck with it.
Uncertainty:	how big? what will it look like?
Risk:	yes! all the above.
Expertise:	can we cope with the lager louts?

If we must persist with the application, we have no choice but to try to soothe the locals. (We change the Action as well as the Audience.) And there are some clues in the above SCORE, STALL and FAILURE analysis.

10A Form for: Cheapway superstore – consultation of locals

1. **Aims** (operational objective)
   get Upper Nimby to agree planning application.
2. **Action** (desired effect of the communication)
   meeting to consult.
3. **Author** (sender of the communication)
   Cheapway managing director. tribe = supermarket chain/responsible planners/"green". aims = obtain planning permission/approval from Upper Nimby.
4. **Audience (recipients of the communication)**
   Upper Nimby Parish Council. tribe = PC/Upper Nimby. aims = no disturbance/be seen to represent residents adequately.
5. **Affinity** (relationship between author and audience)
   selling. "Let us help you preserve your village."
6. **Angle** (point of view to be adopted)
   audience.
7. **Argument** (supporting reasoning)

Synergistic: hear our plans. chance for you to comment.
Compatible: this is how we all like to do business.
Opportune: we have to submit planning application soon.
Rewarding: you can make suggestions which we'll listen to.
Easy: just turn up.
Suspicion: we'll bring witness from Lower Soldham who'll vouch for our integrity.
Theology: none.
Aberration: none.
Linkage: no obligation on either side.
Low priority: application is imminent.
Funding: no cost to you.
Abasement: none. my regional director will be there.
Investment: none.
Lock-in: none. no commitment on your part.
Uncertainty: we'll tell you our future plans.
Risk: none.
Expertise: none.

    intro.
        need for new superstore in the area.
        no other suitable sites.
        need to boost employment in the area.
        we are committed to serve needs of whole community.
    suggest meeting.
        we'll explain plans.
        what we did in Lower Soldham.
        listen to your suggestions.

8. **Appraisal** (checkpoint)
   OK.
9. **Articulation** (how the communication is expressed)
   short friendly letter.
10. **Appearance** (physical appearance of the communication)
    company letterhead.

☆ CHEAPWAY ☆

Head Office: Grimford Road, Slough, Berks.

Major F. Short,
Chairman,
Upper Nimby Parish Council,
Upper Nimby,
Bucks.   October 25th, 1993

Dear Sir,

As you may have heard, we are planning to build a new Cheapway
superstore in Upper Nimby.

Our research has shown that there is a need for this type of amenity
within the Ruffshod & Blowham areas, and, after long deliberation, we
have selected the site at Old Farm as being the most suitable. No other
site offers the same convenience to shoppers, while at the same time
providing extensive free car parking facilities.

The opening of the store will also create a number of new jobs locally.

Cheapway, however, is committed to serve the needs of the entire
community and to adopt best practices in respect of environmental
issues. As a matter of policy, we make every effort to consult those
residents who are most likely to feel affected.

On behalf of Cheapway, therefore, I would like to invite Upper Nimby
Parish Council and any interested residents to a meeting in order to
give the matter a full airing before we submit a formal planning
application.

At the meeting, our regional director will make a full presentation of
our plans. A scale model will be on display, and this will show how we
will screen the site and preserve the appearance of the surrounding
area. Maps will illustrate the traffic flows to and from the store.

We will also invite the chairman of the Lower Soldham Parish
Council to address the meeting. As you know, the new store in Lower
Soldham has been in operation for two years now, and he will tell you
about the very effective steps we took to minimise the impact of the
new store there.

Naturally, we will listen carefully to any other ideas you may have to
keep any disturbance to a minimum.

We are confident you will be reassured by our plans, and that you
will feel able to support this important addition to the shopping
amenities in the area.

I will call you within a few days to discuss our invitation and to
finalise details.

Yours faithfully,

Mike Trolly, Managing Director.

This time, we have gone for an achievable Action with an Audience which is going to be highly influential. Our company's budget will doubtless include provision for a new road which will relieve the traffic through the village itself. There could also be some 'planning gain' (bribing the local residents rather than the planning officers.) This might take the form of paying for renovating the village hall or cricket pavilion. (We'll let the cricketers fight it out with the Morris Dancers as to which has highest priority!)

One danger is that the chairman of Lower Soldham Parish Council might come out with something we would rather he didn't, but on the whole the independent witness should do a great deal to dispel suspicion. Even if we do have something to hide, we can rest assured the residents of Upper Nimby will already have researched it for themselves.

CASE 5

You are co-author of a book entitled Manage The Message. *You have to write an Introduction which will persuade the casual bookstall browser to buy it.*

Although a "Unified Field Theory" of interpersonal motivational techniques remains elusive ...

"We weren't looking for one anyway."

... the authors of this book have successfully synthesised a set of methodologies which are intended as systematic aids to the construction of communications in a contemporary commercial context ...

"C-c-c-crikey!"

The theoretical provenance is authoritative, encompassing, for example, Karpmann's Triangles (albeit extensively modified); the outcome of intensive investigation by the authors of the potential application of Thom's Catastrophe Theory to the discipline of marketing;

"It's a blooming disaster already!"

... which has in turn been further refined during decades of original research into decision-making behaviour.

The aspiring communicator is advised to study this work with diligence.

"Now where did we see that Jeffrey Archer book?"

The suggested solution starts back on page 1 of the book ...

10A Form for: Introduction to Manage The Message

1. **Aims** (operational objective)
   improve persuasive writing skills.
2. **Action** (desired effect of the communication)
   reader to buy the book.
3. **Author** (sender of the communication)
   BDT and JEB. tribes = management/sales/marketing/research/ training/
   writing. aims = sell book.
4. **Audience** (recipients of the communication)
   business management. aims = achieve business objectives/improve
   communication skills/raise personal profile.
5. **Affinity** (relationship between author and audience)
   selling = "Let us help you manage your messages."
6. **Angle** (point of view to be adopted)
   audience.
7. **Argument** (supporting reasoning)

Synergistic:	can be used for meetings and phone calls.
Compatible:	helps people like you do your job.
Opportune:	any time is a good time.
Rewarding:	achieve aims. improve image, self-confidence.
Easy:	simple, practical techniques.
Suspicion:	authors are experienced managers/communicators.
Theology:	none.
Aberration:	no.
Linkage:	none.
Low priority:	should be high priority.
Funding:	very little!
Abasement:	on the contrary.
Investment:	builds on your other skills.
Lock-in	your decision to use techniques or not.
Uncertainty:	writing not about to go out of style.
Risk:	only the price of the book.
Expertise:	very simple to understand and apply.

   objectives
       develop persuasive arguments
       express them effectively
   teaches new skills
       persuasion needed rather than coercion
       effective writing
       MTM combines the two
   spin-offs
       new confidence, higher profile
       also good for meetings, phone calls
       but not teach stereotyped English, manipulation.

8. **Appraisal** (checkpoint)
   OK.
9. **Articulation** (how the communication is expressed)
   entertaining, easy to read (Goblin and graphics)
10. **Appearance** (physical appearance of the communication)
    publisher's house style.

Appendix

"Meet, phone or write" decision matrix

10A Form

SCORE, STALL and FAILURE form

Affinity Model

Meet, Phone or Write?

The following is a rough and ready "Decision Matrix" which will serve as a quick guide to which medium to use. The table ignores all instances when all three methods could be used, and concentrates on cases when one or two of them are advised.

Bear in mind that a "perfect fit" may not be possible. A written report, for example, may need to be backed up with a meeting or phone call, and vice versa.

	M	P	W
Long distance?		✓	✓
One-to-many?	✓		✓
One-to-very many?			✓
Show commitment?	✓	✓	
Seeking clarification?	✓	✓	
Discuss and explore?	✓	✓	
Urgent answer needed?	✓	✓	
Considered response needed?			✓
Complex argument?			✓
Visible evidence?	✓		✓
Audible/tangible evidence?	✓		
Language problems?			✓
Permanent record?			✓
Off-the-record?	✓	✓	

10A Form for:

1. **Aims** (operational objective)

2. **Action** (desired effect of the communication)

3. **Author** (sender of the communication)

4. **Audience** (recipients of the communication)

5. **Affinity** (relationship between author and audience)

6. **Angle** (point of view to be adopted)

7. **Argument** (supporting reasoning)

8. **Appraisal** (checkpoint)

9. **Articulation** (how the communication is expressed)

10. **Appearance** (physical appearance of the communication)

SSF Form for:

Synergistic:

Compatible:

Opportune:

Rewarding:

Easy:

Suspicion:

Theology:

Aberration:

Linkage:

Low priority:

Funding:

Abasement:

Investment:

Lock-in:

Uncertainty:

Risk:

Expertise:

© 1992   Bryan D. Thresher and James E. Biggin

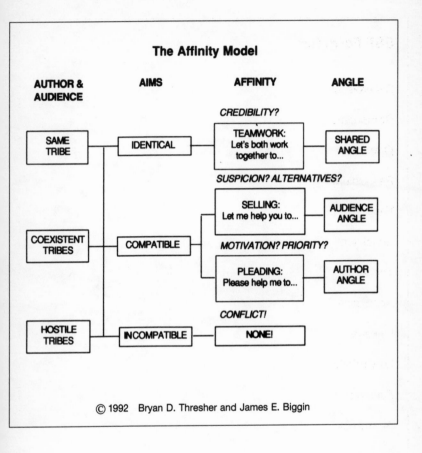

The Affinity Model